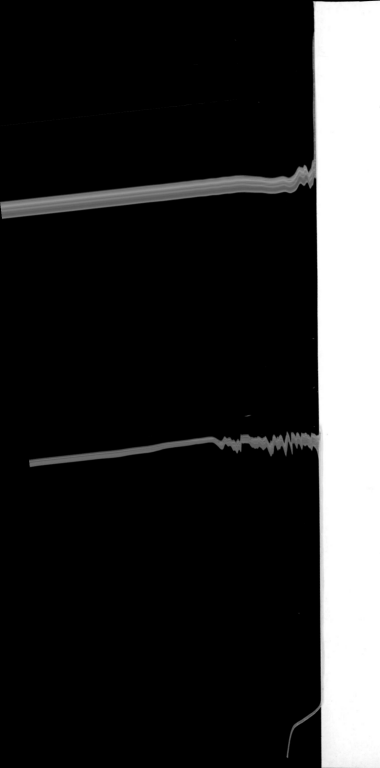

WHEN CHRIST COMES
AND COMES AGAIN

WHEN CHRIST COMES
AND COMES AGAIN

by

T. F. TORRANCE

Wipf & Stock
PUBLISHERS
Eugene, Oregon

Wipf and Stock Publishers
199 W 8th Ave, Suite 3
Eugene, OR 97401

When Christ Comes and Comes Again
By Torrance, Thomas F.
Copyright©1957 by Torrance, Thomas F.
ISBN: 1-57910-009-0
Publication date 11/26/1996
Previously published by Eerdmans, 1957

PREFACE

In this work sixteen sermons preached in parish churches in Scotland, in college and school chapels, and over the radio, have been rewritten for reading and in order to bring out more fully the theological content of evangelism. As written they are, for the most part, much longer, and of course more theological, than when they were preached. They have largely been shorn of their character of direct address as well as of illustrative and literary material.

The specific purpose of publication is two-fold, to meet many requests to have them in print, and also to offer, if only in a small way, some doctrinal material for the use of those actively engaged in the work of evangelism, as well as of the ordinary reading public in our congregations which increasingly demand a more thoughtful presentation of the Christian message.

It is one of the principal tasks of the theologian in each generation to bring the preaching of the Church to the bar of the Word of God and to test its adequacy as a faithful presentation of the message and teaching of the New Testament. In the rising tide of evangelism today it is important that the content of evangelistic proclamation should be tested and examined in this way. But the theologian cannot do that properly unless he is prepared at the same time positively to show what the content of the evangelical message of the Church should be as he sees it. A small contribution to this latter task is offered in this book, but offered only that the theologian's understanding of evangelism may in turn receive criticism from the evangelists themselves, for it is only in such mutual impartation of help that we can be of real service together in the Gospel.

There are aspects of modern preaching which give rise to great anxiety, the temptation of the popular preacher to build the faith of the congregation on his own personality, to parade his knowledge of modern literature, to feed his people with constant diagnosis of the various maladies of our time instead of with the substance of the Gospel, to allow an existentialist decision to oust from their central place in the Gospel the mighty acts of God in Christ, and so to give the people anthropology instead of Christology, or to preach the Church instead of Christ in His Church and so to give the congregation the traditions of men instead of Incarnation, Atonement, Resurrection, Ascension, and Advent. A sheep lost in a snowstorm may eke out its life a little longer by feeding upon its own wool, but the Church cannot live very long by feeding upon its own experience or conventions instead of the Body and Blood of Christ.

This is not, however, a book about preaching but a book presenting some of the material that should be preached. It does not claim by any means to present the whole Gospel, for there are many important aspects of the Gospel not found or stressed in these pages, and very little about the whole sphere of Christian service in love and witness. These particular sermons have been selected because they deal with themes that are found on the lips of evangelists, but they have been enlarged in a plain unadorned manner to set forth an exposition of these themes in a way which appears to be more Biblical and more properly balanced with the emphases of the New Testament.

I have had particularly in mind throughout a frequent failure in modern preaching and evangelism to hold together in a proper unity the following: what God has done for us in Christ, and our experience of Christ; the sacramental "moments" and the evangelical "moments" in the life of faith; God's gracious election and our free human decision; the faithfulness of God and the response of our faith toward Him, and so on. One of the greatest difficulties we have to meet here is the growth and establishment of many conventional ways of presenting the Gospel which have no Biblical foundation but which are unconsciously used as canons for determining and judging whether what is proclaimed is evangelical. Too often the Word of God is bound in the fetters and techniques of an "evangelical tradition" which is man-made and does not derive from the Gospel itself, and can only succeed in making important elements of the Word of none effect.

If this book can help evangelists and ministers to examine and rethink the content of their proclamation in order to let the Word of the Gospel have free course in their ministry, and if it can be of any humble service in imparting to the hungry something of the Bread of Life, it will amply serve the purpose of its publication. But it is my hope that it may provoke others to do much better and more fully what is attempted so inadequately here.

In rewriting these chapters I have been deeply conscious throughout how very much I owe to my own teachers in Edinburgh, the late H. R. Mackintosh and William Manson, both to their lectures and to their books. Some readers will recognise thoughts and expressions which I have absorbed from the commentaries and sermons of John Calvin which I read regularly as a parish minister in the preparation of sermons, along with modern critical commentaries, and frequently the homiletical expositions of Alexander MacLaren (whom Mackintosh used to call "the prince of preachers"). In the first chapter I am indebted to the late F. W. Camfield (*The Collapse of Doubt*) and to the Rev. C. E. B. Cranfield (in *Essays in Christology for Karl Barth*, ed. by T. H. L.

Parker) for several citations. The Editors of *Biblical Theology* (Belfast) and of *The Cambridge Review* have kindly allowed me to include material which had already appeared in their journals.

Easter, 1957.

New College,
      Edinburgh.

CONTENTS

I

THE ADVENT OF THE REDEEMER

CHAPTER I

WHEN CHRIST COMES TO THE WORLD

"And as he went forth out of the temple, one of his disciples saith unto him, Master, behold, what manner of stones and what manner of buildings! And Jesus said unto him, Seest thou these great buildings? there shall not be left here one stone upon another, which shall not be thrown down.

"And as he sat on the mount of Olives over against the temple, Peter and James and John and Andrew asked him privately, Tell us, when shall these things be? and what shall be the sign when these things are all about to be accomplished? And Jesus began to say unto them, Take heed that no man lead you astray. Many shall come in my name, saying, I am he; and shall lead many astray. And when ye shall hear of wars and rumours of wars, be not troubled: these things must needs come to pass; but the end is not yet. For nation shall rise against nation, and kingdom against kingdom: there shall be earthquakes in divers places; there shall be famines: these things are the beginning of travail.

"But take heed to yourselves: for they shall deliver you up to councils; and in synagogues shall ye be beaten; and before governors and kings shall ye stand for my sake, for a testimony unto them. And the gospel must first be preached unto all the nations. And when they lead you to judgement, and deliver you up, be not anxious beforehand what ye shall speak: but whatsoever shall be given you in that hour, that speak ye: for it is not ye that speak, but the Holy Ghost. And brother shall deliver up brother to death, and the father his child; and children shall rise up against parents, and cause them to be put to death. And ye shall be hated of all men for my name's sake: but he that endureth to the end, the same shall be saved.

"But when ye shall see the abomination of desolation standing where he ought not (let him that readeth understand), then let them that are in Judaea flee unto the mountains: and let him that is on the housetop not go down, nor enter in, to take anything out of his house: and let him that is in the field not return back to take his cloke. But woe unto them that are with child and to them that give suck in those days! And pray ye that it be not in the winter. For those days shall be tribulation, such as there hath not been the like from the beginning of the creation which God created until now, and never shall be. And except the Lord had shortened the days, no flesh would have been saved: but for the elect's sake, whom he chose, he shortened the days. And then if any man shall say unto you, Lo, here is the Christ; or, Lo, there; believe it not: for there shall arise false Christs and false prophets, and shall shew signs and wonders, that they may lead astray, if possible, the elect. But take ye heed: behold, I have told you all things beforehand."

Mark 13, 1-23.

"The former treatise I made, O Theophilus, concerning all that Jesus began both to do and to teach, until the day in which he was received up, after that he had given commandment through the Holy Ghost unto the apostles whom he had chosen: to whom he also shewed himself alive after his passion by many proofs, appearing unto them by the space of forty days, and speaking the things concerning the kingdom of God: and, being assembled together with them, he charged them not to depart from Jerusalem, but to wait for the promise of the Father, which, said he, ye heard from me: for John indeed baptized with water; but ye shall be baptized with the Holy Ghost not many days hence.

"They therefore, when they were come together, asked him, saying, Lord, dost thou at this time restore the kingdom to Israel? And he said unto them, It is not for you to know times or seasons, which the Father hath set within his own authority. But ye shall receive power, when the Holy Ghost is come upon you: and ye shall be my witnesses both in Jerusalem, and in all Judaea and Samaria, and unto the uttermost part of the earth. And when he had said these things, as they were looking, he was taken up; and a cloud received him out of their sight. And while they were looking stedfastly into heaven as he went, behold two men stood by them in white apparel; which also said, Ye men of Galilee, why stand ye looking into heaven? this Jesus, which was received up from you into heaven, shall so come in like manner as ye beheld him going into heaven. Then returned they unto Jerusalem from the mount called Olivet, which is nigh unto Jerusalem, a sabbath day's journey off."

Acts 1, 1-12.

"This same Jesus, which is taken up from you into heaven, shall so come in like manner as ye have seen him go into heaven."

Acts I, II.

This same Jesus will actually come again—that is the exciting and exhilarating message we consider especially at Advent. Even when throughout the Advent season we think mostly of the birth of Jesus at Bethlehem, the message of Advent is that He who was born to be King will come again as the King of Glory to take up His power and to reign over the nations and over all creation. That is not a message that can be confined to a few weeks in the year, for the whole life of the Church is governed by it. Therefore all our thought and all our work must be allowed to come under the impact of Advent.

This same Jesus will come again! Who is this Jesus? He is the Jesus of Bethlehem, the Jesus of Calvary, the Jesus of the Resurrection. It is identically the same Jesus as the historical Jesus who will come again. Let us think about the significance of that.

This same Jesus is the Jesus of Bethlehem. He is the eternal Son of God who entered into our human life and was born at Bethlehem into a human family as the child of Mary. And He was called JESUS, which means *Saviour*, because He came to save His people from their sins—that was the kind of King He was born to be: not the kind of king who is infinitely exalted over our human history quite untouched by its desperate perplexity and hopeless misery, but the King who has Himself come into our human situation by becoming a man among us, come into the midst of our responsibilities and guilt, in order to take it all on His own shoulders, and so to stand surety for us within our frailty and corruption and lostness. He came in fact to share to the full our human life that we might share His eternal life. He came to be the life of our life and so to redeem us and reconcile us to God against whom we have been rebels and sinners. That is the breath-taking good news

B

of Christmas, that in the birth of Jesus the eternal God has bound Himself up with us in the same bundle of life, that God has embroiled Himself for ever with our human history with all its sin and failure and guilt, so that now the whole of our human destiny depends entirely upon Jesus. It is this same Jesus who will actually come again.

This same Jesus is also the Jesus of Calvary. He is God Himself who has stooped down to bear our sin, and to take our judgment upon Himself in order to do away with our sin and to forgive us and to release us from our guilty past. What a baffling creature man is! It is the glory of man that he has a history, a history of magnificent achievements, but man has also a past, a wicked past. That is the fateful and demonic thing about man: he has a past which he cannot undo, a past which is not dead but actively alive, for as surely as a rudder steers a ship from behind, so the past steers man's course through history. And yet that is not a good analogy—we can manipulate the rudder of a ship, but we cannot manipulate the past; we cannot change or alter it in the slightest.

That is worth thinking about more fully. Let us take the case of two young people who get married, and then later in fearful tragedy are divorced. Divorce does not and cannot alter the fact that though they were virgins when they got married they are no longer virgins: each has permanently changed the being of the other in a way that no power in all the universe can undo. So it is with sin against God and against man: nothing can alter the fact of sin; it enters permanently into the past and remains there; no matter how much it is hated and regretted, it cannot be recalled. That is "the terrible grief, the awful damage, the unappeasable agony" of man's past.[1] That is the horror and curse not only of every man but of mankind, of the history of the nations. He who could deal with this, who could bear the judgment

[1] F. W. Camfield, *The Collapse of Doubt* (Lutterworth Press, 1945), p. 92.

and wrath that fall upon man because of his sin, he who could cancel guilt, undo the past, take away its curse, and set man entirely free and give him a new life, he would be the mightiest power in heaven and earth. He would be King of Kings and Lord of Lords, the only real Saviour. But that is just who Jesus is, the Man of Calvary, for He is God Almighty come down into our sinful history to take upon Himself man's guilt and shame. He even entered into man's death, where judgment upon man's past is piled up high against him. He took all that upon Himself for man's sake, that by bringing it upon His own Self God might bring man pardon, absolution and salvation. And so the Cross stands in the midst of human history, for in the crucified Jesus God Himself has penetrated into the fateful destiny of history, into its innermost tragedy and curse, and now He holds the keys of death and hell in His hands. It is this Jesus who bears the sin of the world, this same Jesus who will come again.

This same Jesus is also the Jesus of the Resurrection. It belongs to the very essence of the Christian faith that Jesus rose again from the dead in body, in the fulness of His humanity. If the resurrection of Jesus is not a literal and actual fact, then the powers of death remain unbroken and sin and guilt have triumphed after all, even over Jesus—then we are yet in our sins and without any hope whatsoever. Everything depends upon the actual physical resurrection of Jesus. Jesus is not dead. He is not a ghost. He did not disappear into the thin air of spirit. He rose again as Man, and opened up a way of salvation for us men and women of flesh and blood. Far from being held captive by the bonds of sin and death, far from being made a prisoner for ever by entering into a guilty past that cannot be undone, Jesus Christ did the impossible: He snapped the bonds of sin and guilt; He broke open the prison-house of the past and shattered the power of death by His resurrection from the grave. And now He is alive for ever more on the other side of corruption and death and judgment, in the life of the new creation. It is this resurrected and triumphant Jesus, this same Jesus, who will come again.

Can we wonder, then, that the Early Church was tense with excitement at the thought that this same Jesus would come again? When He comes He will come with the destiny of men and nations in His hands; He will come to fulfil His judgment upon all evil and to release history from the tragedy of guilt that no man can undo, and He will make all things new. He will come as the King of Glory to take His power and reign over a renewed creation. That will be the Kingdom of Peace to which there will be no end.

But why does He postpone His coming, and what will be the sign of His coming? Those questions were already asked by people in New Testament times, and they are still being asked. What is the answer to them? Why does Jesus postpone His coming? Why has He already postponed His coming back to the world for nearly 1900 years?

In His first Advent Jesus came not with glory and power but in grace and humiliation. He came in such a way as to enter into our guilty human life and to heal it *from within* by His suffering and death on the Cross. God could have destroyed all evil by a single stroke of His hand, but far from saving or healing man that would have destroyed mankind altogether along with all sin and evil. Therefore God took a different course altogether. In His infinite mercy and patience He stooped down in Jesus Christ, and entered into our sinful human life with all its proud self-sufficiency and incurable self-will, and when in enmity against God and in proud rebellion against His grace man crucified Jesus on the Cross, God took that Cross and made it the instrument for the healing of the nations. And so it is by the same Cross preached among all nations that God in Christ patiently seeks and saves the lost. It is because He wants all men to be saved that

Christ has planted His Cross in the midst of history and through His Cross is still at work in the midst of history, so that in a very real sense all history is gathered into the passion of Christ. He has postponed His coming in power and glory because He wants to rule over the hearts of men from His Cross; He has postponed His coming in might and judgment because He wants first to meet with every man at His Cross, there to release him from his sin and guilt, there to ask of him the love of his heart, and there to remake him as God's dear child. But this time which God has given for the preaching of the Gospel to all nations, time for repentance and decision, does not go on for ever. It will have an end, for Jesus Christ will return in power to fulfil what He has promised, to undo the past, and to make all things new. Those who refuse to repent, who still cling to their past, will themselves be undone, for they will come under the judgment of Christ by which He will release His creation from the curse and tragedy of evil. But to all who repent, who have learned to take up His Cross and follow Him, Jesus Christ will return not only to judge but to set them at liberty and to make all things new.

When Jesus will come again in power and glory to take up His reign we do not know. He has told us that it will be sudden, and just when we expect it least, like a thief in the night. But there are signs of His coming. They are not signs that tell us when He will come, but signs and pledges telling us unmistakably that the end will come, as surely as day follows night, and that world-history will be brought to a close. The signs make it more and more clear that "the only thing that holds back the end of history is God's patience that waits to give men time to hear the Gospel and believe."[1] But they are signs that direct our eyes forward to the coming of Jesus, and keep us on the tip-toe of expectation.

[1] C. E. B. Cranfield, *Essays in Christology for Karl Barth* (ed. by T. H. L. Parker), p. 90. Lutterworth Press, 1956.

We live today in such a period of history. There have been wars and rumours of wars, and men's hearts fail with fear of the calamities that may come upon the earth, but the end is not yet. It is almost like the stillness before a storm, when the birds flap their wings in frightened anxiety, and all nature seems to hold its breath, waiting for the first streak of lightning and the stroke of thunder that will change the whole atmosphere. God gives us signs in history like that, not in order to predict the time of Christ's coming but to keep us faithful to our task of preaching the Gospel to all nations,[1] and serving of our fellow-men in acts of unstinting love. He who is reminded by these signs to be faithful to his task will not hang about waiting for something to happen, but will go forth to meet his coming Lord by pouring out his own life in the service of the Gospel. And he who in that service has learned to love his fellow-men, to understand and share their suffering, and to long for their redemption, will be thrown back again and again upon the glorious hope of Advent: *This same Jesus will come*, and he too will pray fervently like the Early Christians, *Even so, come, Lord Jesus*.

CHAPTER II

WHEN CHRIST COMES TO THE CHURCH

"But in those days, after that tribulation, the sun shall be darkened, and the moon shall not give her light, and the stars shall be falling from heaven, and the powers that are in the heavens shall be shaken. And then shall they see the Son of man coming in clouds with great power and glory. And then shall he send forth the angels, and shall gather together his elect from the four winds, from the uttermost part of the earth to the uttermost part of heaven.

[1] C. Cranfield, op. cit., p. 91.

"Now from the fig tree learn her parable: when her branch is now become tender, and putteth forth its leaves, ye know that the summer is nigh; even so also, when ye see these things coming to pass, know ye that he is nigh, even at the doors. Verily I say unto you, This generation shall not pass away, until all these things be accomplished. Heaven and earth shall pass away: but my words shall not pass away. But of that day or of that hour knoweth no one, not even the angels in heaven, neither the Son, but the Father. Take ye heed, watch and pray: for ye know not when the time is. It is as when a man, sojourning in another country, having left his house, and given authority to his servants, to each one his work, commanded also the porter to watch. Watch therefore: for ye know not when the lord of the house cometh, whether at even, or at midnight, or at cock-crowing, or in the morning; lest coming suddenly he find you sleeping. And what I say unto you I say unto all, Watch."   Mark 13, 24-37.

"The Revelation of Jesus Christ, which God gave him to shew unto his servants, even the things which must shortly come to pass: and he sent and signified it by his angel unto his servant John; who bare witness of the word of God, and of the testimony of Jesus Christ, even of all things that he saw. Blessed is he that readeth, and they that hear the words of the prophecy, and keep the things that are written therein: for the time is at hand.

"John to the seven churches which are in Asia: Grace to you and peace, from him which is and which was and which is to come; and from the seven Spirits which are before his throne; and from Jesus Christ, who is the faithful witness, the first-born of the dead, and the ruler of the kings of the earth. Unto him that loveth us and loosed us from our sins by his blood; and made us to be a kingdom, to be priests unto his God and Father; to him be the glory and the dominion for ever and ever. Amen. Behold, he cometh with the clouds; and every eye shall see him, and they which pierced him; and all the tribes of the earth shall mourn over him. Even so, Amen.

"I am the Alpha and the Omega, saith the Lord God, which is and which was and which is to come, the Almighty.

"I John, your brother and partaker with you in the tribulation and kingdom and patience which are in Jesus, was in the isle that is called Patmos, for the word of God and the testimony of Jesus. I was in the Spirit on the Lord's day, and I heard behind me a great voice, as of a trumpet saying, What thou seest, write in a book, and send it to the seven churches; unto Ephesus, and unto Smyrna, and unto Pergamum, and unto Thyatira, and unto Sardis, and unto Philadelphia, and unto Laodicea. And I turned to see the voice which spake with me. And having turned I saw seven golden candlesticks; and in the midst of the candlesticks one like unto a son of man, clothed with a garment down to the foot, and girt about at the breasts with a golden girdle. And his head and his hair were white as white wool, white as snow; and his eyes were as a flame of fire; and his feet like unto burnished brass, as if it had been refined in a furnace; and his voice as the voice of many waters. And he had in his right hand seven stars: and out of his mouth proceeded a sharp two-edged sword: and his countenance was as the sun shineth in his strength. And when I saw him, I fell at his feet as one dead. And he laid his right hand upon me, saying, Fear not; I am the first and the last, and the Living one; and I was dead, and behold, I am alive for evermore, and I have the keys of death and of Hades. Write therefore the things which thou sawest, and the things which are, and the things which shall come to pass hereafter; the mystery of the seven stars which thou sawest in my right hand, and the seven golden candlesticks. The seven stars are the angels of the seven churches: and the seven candlesticks are seven churches."

Revelation 1, 1-20.

"Behold, I stand at the door and knock: if any man hear my voice and open the door, I will come in to him, and will sup with him, and he with me."

The Revelation of St. John the Divine 3, 20.

Who is this who knocks at the door of the Church and whose voice is heard inside the Church?

St. John himself heard this same voice speaking to him like a trumpet, and he tells us: "And I turned to see the voice of him that spoke with me, and being turned I saw one like unto the Son of Man." It was none other than Jesus standing in the midst of His Church, Jesus His beloved Master and Saviour, who had been crucified but who had risen again and ascended to God the Father. But let us note the way in which St. John describes this Jesus:—"His head and His hairs were white as wool, as white as snow; and his eyes were as a flame of fire, and his feet like unto fine brass, as if they burned in a furnace; and his voice as the voice of many waters. And he had in his right hand seven stars: and out of his mouth went a sharp two-edged sword: and his countenance was as the sun shineth in his strength. And when I saw him, I fell at his feet as dead. And he laid his right hand upon me, saying unto me, Fear not: I am the first and the last: I am he that liveth, and was dead, and behold, I am alive for ever more, Amen; and I have the keys of hell and death."

What an astonishing description to give of Jesus! It was the same Jesus of whom we read in the Gospels, the lowly Jesus of Bethlehem and Nazareth, the Jesus of Galilee, the friend of sinners and the physician of the poor, the Jesus on whose breast John leaned at the Last Supper, and it is, I believe, the same John, the nearest of all the disciples to the heart of Jesus, who writes about his vision. But now when John saw this same beloved Jesus in the unveiled glory of His transcendent majesty, he fell down before Him in breathless awe and unrestrained adoration. And then out of the heart of that burning vision there came the unmistakable voice of Jesus and the familiar touch of His hand. "Fear not, John, I am alive. I was dead, but now I live for ever, and I have absolute control over all the powers of darkness and evil."

What had happened to make John see Jesus like that? It was the resurrection of Jesus and His ascension to the throne of God Almighty. Though humbled for a season, Jesus was now glorified with the glory which He had with the Father before the world was. He was so transfigured in the sublime light of His Deity, that when John saw Him he could hardly find words to describe Him. That is how Jesus appears to a man who has seen Him in the power of His resurrection. That is what Jesus becomes for the man who has been forgiven and redeemed, and that is how Jesus is to be seen and worshipped as the exalted Saviour and Lord. It is the same

Jesus, but now shining unveiled in the lustre of uncreated Light.

That light John had seen for the first time in Galilee, when he thought of it as the glory of the only-begotten of the Father full of grace and truth. Now he speaks of it as a blinding reality, a countenance as the sun shines in its strength, eyes like a flame of fire and feet like burnished brass as if they burned in a furnace. No wonder the Old Testament saints used to say that they could not see God and live, for God is a consuming fire. And yet that is just how we all must see God even in the face of Jesus Christ, if we are to be saved by Him: in the full blaze of His Holiness and Majesty.

Until we have seen Jesus like that, we have not seen Him in His full reality. We have seen Him only in the reality of His fleshly garments with which in His mercy He veiled His divine glory, and have not seen Jesus who is the Christ, the Son of the living God. We cannot see Jesus just by piecing together picturesque historical detail about Him. Flesh and blood cannot reveal Jesus. Something else must happen. We must allow the sublime majesty of Jesus to break in upon our vision. Jesus must be transfigured before our very eyes. It is through His Cross that He pierces like that into our souls, and then it is in the power of His resurrection that He stands before us, shows the wounds in His hands and side, and says "Peace be unto you"—and, like St. Thomas, we can only fall before Him and say, "My Lord and my God."

That is the Jesus who stands at the door and knocks, and whose voice is to be heard inside the Church. It is the knocking of the Advent King upon the outer structure of the Church in the world—Jesus the King of glory who is already on His way, who is already at the door. It is *His* voice that we hear today inside the Church. "If any man will open the door I will come in to him, and sup with him and he with me." Until Jesus Christ comes again with all His power and glory to judge the quick and the dead, His living voice is to be heard in the Church, speaking to us out of the pages of the Bible.

None of the Gospels ever gives us the slightest hint about what Jesus looked like. They tell us nothing at all about His appearance, but they do speak about His *voice*, and they tell us of the amazement of the multitudes who wondered at the gracious words that fell from His lips. "Never man spake like this man." When Jesus rose again from the dead, even Mary Magdalene did not recognise Him until Jesus spoke to her by name, and then immediately she recognised Jesus by His voice. We recall also how the two disciples walking to Emmaus on Easter evening did not recognise Jesus when He joined their company, although the words He spoke to them made their hearts burn within them.

That is just how it is today. We cannot see Jesus, for He has withdrawn Himself from our sight; and we will not see Him face to face until He comes again—but we *can hear* His *voice* speaking to us in the midst of the Church on earth. That is the perpetual miracle of the Bible, for it is the inspired instrument through which the voice of Christ is still to be heard. Jesus Christ was the Word of God made flesh, the still small voice of God embodied in our humanity, and it is that same Word, and that same voice, that is given to the Church in the Bible. It is by that voice that the Church in all ages is called into being, and upon that Word of God that the Church is founded. The Church is, in fact, the Community of the Voice of God, for it is the business of the Church to open the Bible and let the voice of Christ speaking in and through it be heard all over the world. It is the mission of the Church to carry the Bible to all nations, and to plant it in every home in the land, and by preaching and teaching, and the witness of its members, to make the Word of God audible, so that the living Voice of Jesus Christ the Saviour of men may be heard by every man and woman and child.

That is why St. Paul speaks of the Church as the earthen vessel filled with the heavenly treasure of the Gospel. Yes, the Church on earth is very earthen, like the seven Churches to which St. John writes in the book of Revelation, all of which have their failures and mistakes and some of them are grievous sins. And yet the Lord Jesus Christ is pleased to dwell in the midst of this earthen and erring Church, and to call it His Body, and to use it as the medium through which He seeks and saves the lost, through which He bestows His healing and salvation and peace, and through which He summons the world to repent before He comes to judge and renew His creation.

Let us think again about the Voice of Jesus that is to be heard in the Church. St. John tells us that out of the mouth of Jesus there goes a sharp two-edged sword. The words spoken by the Voice of Jesus are words that cut both ways. They are words that cut and cleanse and heal; but they are also words that cut and judge and consume. To understand that let us go back to the Gospels and listen to the voice of Jesus speaking. Never have there been words so tender and full of compassion as the words of Jesus to the contrite sinner, to the lost and helpless. "Come unto me all ye that labour and are heavy laden, and I will give you rest." "Son, thy sins be forgiven thee." "Daughter, go in peace; thy faith hath made thee whole." That is the Voice of God that cuts away our guilt and sets us free from the burden of our sins. But never have such sharp words been spoken as were spoken by Jesus to the proud and the self-righteous, words that cut into men's hearts exposing their secret hypocrisy and shame—words that carried the fire of judgment. No wonder St. John spoke of Jesus as having eyes like a flame of fire, eyes that search the heart consuming evil with its flame.

It is the same voice of Jesus that is to be heard today in His Church on earth, for it is to this Church that He has given, in the Bible, the Sword of the Spirit which is the Word of God. And it is to this Church that Jesus has said: "I give unto you the keys of the Kingdom of heaven, and whatsoever you shall bind on earth shall be bound in heaven; and whatsoever you shall loose on earth shall be loosed in heaven." "Whosesoever sins you remit, they are remitted unto them, and whosesoever sins you retain they are retained."

What does that mean? It is the mission of the Church to unlock the Bible, and to let the voice of Christ loose upon the world. It is the mission of the Church to confess that Jesus Christ is the Son of the living God, and by preaching the Gospel of the Cross to bring all men face to face with Jesus Christ challenging them to confess Him as Saviour and Lord. And so it is the mission of the Church to proclaim the Truth of the Gospel and to bind it upon the hearts and consciences of men.

Take Martin Luther, for example. Luther opened the long-closed Bible and began to expound to Europe the Christ of the Gospels and the Gospel of justification by free grace, and in so doing he was binding and loosing the consciences of men. No man hears the Gospel without either being loosed from the tyranny of sin and being saved by Christ, or being bound more and more in his conscience and being hardened against Christ and His Gospel.

It is this sharp two-edged sword, the Word of the Gospel, that is put into the mouth of ordinary people in the Church: that is the foolishness of preaching, as St. Paul called it. The preaching of Christ is an offence to some people; it is folly to other people. But to those who are perishing and who believe, it is the very power of God, because through this preaching it is the Christ Himself who knocks at the door, and it is His living voice that demands an answer.

But now we are reminded again that this Christ who comes to the Church in the preaching of the Gospel will come again in power and glory, and when He comes He will call the Church on earth to give an account of its stewardship of the Gospel, and by the two-edged sword of the same Gospel He will both judge and cleanse His Church. What will He say to the Churches which claim to preach reconciliation through the Blood of Christ but refuse to be reconciled to one another? Will He not say that though they preached reconciliation by their lips they acted a lie against it by being divided from one another? What will He say to those who are only concerned for their own comfort and salvation, and not for the poor and needy in all parts of the world? Will He not say: "I was hungry and you did not give me to eat; I was thirsty and you did not give me to drink. Depart from me, for I never knew you"? Let us not forget that He will come in judgment as well as in mercy even to His Church. Listen to His words: "As many as I love, I rebuke and chasten: be zealous therefore, and repent. Behold, I stand at the door and knock: if any man hear my voice and open the door, I will come in to him, and will sup with him, and he with me." Happy the Church that hears that knocking upon its door, and is watching and ready for the coming of the Advent Lord!

Although those words are spoken primarily to the Church, they are also meant to be heard by the individual. Each of us may hear Jesus knocking on the door of his heart, and to each Jesus waits to say: "My son, my daughter, your sins are forgiven. Go in peace."

CHAPTER III

WHEN CHRIST COMES TO
THE INDIVIDUAL

"Now in the sixth month the angel Gabriel was sent from God unto a city of Galilee, named Nazareth, to a virgin betrothed to a man whose name was Joseph, of the house of David; and the virgin's name was Mary. And he came in unto her, and said, Hail, thou that art highly favoured, the Lord is with thee. But she was greatly troubled at the saying, and cast in her mind what manner of salutation this might be. And the angel said unto her, Fear not, Mary: for thou hast found favour with God. And behold, thou shalt conceive in thy womb, and bring forth a son, and shalt call his name Jesus. He shall be great, and shall be called the Son of the Most High: and the Lord God shall give unto him the throne of his father David: and he shall reign over the house of Jacob for ever; and of his kingdom there shall be no end. And Mary said unto the angel, How shall this be, seeing I know not a man? And the angel answered and said unto her, The Holy Ghost shall come upon thee, and the power of the Most High shall overshadow thee: wherefore also that which is to be born shall be called holy, the Son of God. And behold, Elisabeth thy kinswoman, she also hath conceived a son in her old age: and this is the sixth month with her that was called barren. For no word from God shall be void of power. And Mary said, Behold the handmaid of the Lord, be it unto me according to thy word. And the angel departed from her."   Luke 1, 26-38.

"Then shall the kingdom of heaven be likened unto ten virgins, which took their lamps, and went forth to meet the bridegroom. And five of them were foolish, and five were wise. For the foolish, when they took their lamps, took no oil with them: but the wise took oil in their vessels with their lamps. Now while the bridegroom tarried, they all slumbered and slept. But at midnight there is a cry, Behold, the bridegroom! Come ye forth to meet him. Then all those virgins arose, and trimmed their lamps. And the foolish said unto the wise, Give us of your oil; for our lamps are going out. But the wise answered, saying, Peradventure there will not be enough for us and you: go ye rather to them that sell, and buy for yourselves. And while they went away to buy, the bridegroom came; and they that were ready went in with him to the marriage feast: and the door was shut. Afterward came also the other virgins, saying, Lord, Lord, open to us. But he answered and said, Verily I say unto you, I know you not. Watch therefore, for ye know not the day nor the hour."   Matthew 25, 1-13.

"And Mary said, Behold the handmaid of the Lord; be it unto me according to thy word."   Luke 1, 38.

That is the answer of Mary to the angelic announcement that she was to be the virgin-mother of Jesus.

Who would ever have dreamed that the eternal Son of God would come into our world in that surprising way? And yet that is the great miraculous sign that God has placed at the beginning of the earthly life of Jesus. It is the sign of the way which God's love has taken toward us in Christ, but it is also a sign of the way in which Christ still comes to each of us, and a sign pointing to the way in which He, born to be King at Bethlehem, will come again in royal sovereignty and grace.

Recall what happened to Mary. God sent His angel to announce to her the good news, but at his first greeting Mary was troubled and had to be reassured. Then she was told of God's gracious decision, that she was to be the mother of Jesus, the Saviour of the world. But how could that be, for although Mary was engaged to be the bride of Joseph, she was not married? The angel answered that the birth of this holy child was to be the direct work of the Spirit and power of God, for with God nothing is impossible. Then, knowing well what others might think of her as a virgin-mother, but with great humility and sublime joy, Mary gave her answer: "Behold the handmaid of the Lord; be it unto me according to thy word."

And so Jesus was born, the Son of the Highest, born from

above. Jesus Christ was born into this world, not from it. He did not evolve out of humanity. He came into humanity. Jesus is not the product of man, but the Creator of man. He is not just the best human being; He is the Being who cannot be accounted for by the human race at all. Jesus is not man becoming God, but God becoming man—God incarnate, God descending into human flesh, coming into it from outside and from above, in order to be one of us, and to be one with us.

That is the miracle of the Incarnation. That is the good news that continues to be announced to us after all these centuries, and it is just as relevant to us in these fateful times as it ever was. If we cannot see any hope for the world *within* the world, if we cannot see rising out of the distant horizon a day of peace, then let us listen to the message of Advent: God's peace does not come that way. God's peace will certainly come to this distracted earth, but it will come as the dayspring from *on high*, and come as a divine visitation in such a way and at such a time as we think not.

That is the logic of Advent. The miracle of Christmas was in absurd contradiction to the facts, and it still is. Recall again Jesus' own advent message to the disciples, just before His crucifixion. "When ye shall see Jerusalem compassed about with armies, then know that the desolation thereof is nigh. . . . And when these things begin to come to pass, then look up, and lift up your heads; for your redemption draws nigh." That is the logic of Jesus, in sheer contradiction to the terribly black facts of our world: Look *up*, Lift *up* your hearts, for the redemption of the world comes breaking into it from above and beyond all our calculations, and all our scientific "facts", above and beyond all our fears and expectations. The advent of the King of Peace will take us completely by surprise, just as it did in the birth of Jesus of the virgin Mary.

But now what is God's special Word to us as we think of

c

the angel's announcement to Mary and of Mary's answer? It is this: what happened to Mary is the God-given sign of the way in which God comes to us also. Jesus Christ was actually born of the virgin Mary, and in a similar way, in a spiritual way, He wants to be born anew in your hearts, or, to put it the other way round, He wants each of us to be born again in Him.

But how can we be born again? How can we become new beings? Again and again we are told that we must make a decision for Christ, but how can we by our decision bring Christ into our life? Each of us knows quite well that his decision cannot effect anything. Nothing that any of us can do can bring Jesus Christ into his life or make it anew.

But let us think of what happened to Mary. God Almighty made Himself little and entered into Mary's life, and Mary found herself cradling a tiny infant in her arms who was none other than the eternal Son of God. Nothing that Mary could have done, even with the co-operation of Joseph, could have brought about that stupendous fact. The holy child was born through the womb of the virgin Mary, but He came as a pure gift of God from outside the range of human possibilities and above and beyond all human powers. He came to Mary in the midst of her most intimate life and thought; He came in great tenderness and humility, but He came as a pure gift imparted to her from beyond and above herself altogether. Nor was the coming of Jesus Christ into her life the result of her decision—how could she have even that power over her Saviour? The decision had already been made, made by God; and God's gracious decision was announced to her by the angel. Mary's reply was simply: "Behold the handmaid of the Lord; be it unto me according to thy word." She acknowledged the decision that had already been made on her behalf; she let the Word of God happen to her, and Jesus was born of her from above.

That is the good news of Advent announced to you in the Church: that we too are highly favoured of God, that in Jesus Christ God has already made a decision on your behalf, that we are to be His children and that Jesus Christ is your Saviour. The decision has already been taken and it is announced to us in the Gospel.

Take Zacchaeus, for example, that mean and hardhearted extortioner who did not have it in him to be a Christian; he was so enslaved to his miserly greed and so tightly bound by his own selfishness that he was not free to make any decision to follow Jesus even if he wanted to. But then Jesus took him by surprise, and announced to him the good news: "This day I must abide at thy house." Jesus announced that He had already decided to enter into the home and life of Zacchaeus, and then, for the first time, beyond any imaginable possibility, Zacchaeus found himself free to follow Jesus, free and able to have Jesus Christ in his home and his heart: he was able to make a decision for Christ, because Christ had already made a decision on his behalf.

That is the way in which the miracle of Advent still operates in the lives of men. And so God set the miracle of the virgin birth at the very beginning of the Gospel to show us the way that God's love takes with us in all our human frailty and weakness. And that is why Mary's answer to the angel is recorded, as an example of the way we are to respond to God's pure gift of grace in Jesus Christ. "Behold the handmaid of the Lord; be it unto me according to thy word."

It is God's Word that announces to us the good news of our destiny in the divine love, and it is ours to let ourselves be told by God's Word, and to let His Word happen to us. When the Gospel is announced to us, it tells us that long before we can do anything about it, and even before we can know about it, God has set His love upon us and chosen us in Jesus Christ to be His own. It is not ours to imagine that by our own choice or decision we can constitute ourselves Christians, but rather to take refuge from our own frail decisions in God and His firm decision of grace which has already overtaken us in Christ. It is God's steadfast, eternal decision that undergirds our feeble and faltering decisions and enfolds them securely in His own. The whole of our salvation depends upon the faithfulness of God to His own Word, and He does not tire of being faithful. Is it any wonder that Mary said: "Be it unto me according to thy word"?

But now let us remember that when Jesus Christ first came into the world, He came as an individual to an individual in Mary. It is in the same individual way that Christ comes to every one. It is not with God in general that we have to do in the Christian faith, but with the personal God who comes in this particular individual, Jesus, so that in and through Jesus we are each summoned to meet with God individually, and to hear from Him the Word of His love. That is an inescapable fact of the Gospel. We cannot fly for refuge from our own individual responsibilities to other people, or even to the Church; nor can we fly for refuge to God behind the back of Jesus Christ, this individual Jesus Christ who stands in our path and confronts us, for it is only in Him that God comes to meet us. And it is only in Him that we can hear God's decision of love about us. That is how He came to Mary, and that is how now in our day He comes to us—individually.

But if Jesus Christ came into the world as an individual, it is as an individual that He will come again, when every eye shall see Him, and every knee shall bow before Him, and every tongue confess that He is Lord. Each one of us will have to meet Him individually face to face. Turn to the parable Jesus told about the ten virgins who took their lamps and went forth to meet the bridegroom. Five of them were wise, but five were foolish, for they took no oil with their lamps. When they were roused at midnight to go and meet the bridegroom, they all went to trim their lamps, and the foolish said unto the wise, "Give us of your oil; for our lamps are gone out." But that was an impossible request. That kind of light cannot be got from our fellows. There is no possible transfer of light from one man's soul to another man's soul. There we have the awful individuality of each soul before God, and its unshareable personal responsibility. We cannot share our neighbour's oil; we may share his possessions, but not the light of his soul.

There is only one Light that lighteth every man—that is the Light that came into the world with the birth of Jesus, when the dayspring from on high visited us to give light to them that sit in darkness. Each man's soul-light must be kindled directly from that source. That light has shone in all our hearts, as it shone in the lamps of all ten virgins, the foolish as well as the wise. But in the moment of crisis at the advent of the bridegroom, when the virgins hastily trimmed their lamps, in five of them the lights burned brightly for a moment and then flickered out and died altogether. The five foolish virgins were astonished as well as alarmed at seeing their lights go out. It was the last thing they expected. Outwardly there may be no difference between the wise and the foolish, but the truth comes out at the last, in the crisis of the Advent.

Not long after the birth of Jesus the aged Simeon told Mary that her child was set for the fall and rising again of many, a sign that would be spoken against. So it has proved all through history. All men are divided, they are cast down or raised up by God, in accordance with their reaction to the child of Bethlehem. And at the second Advent of this same Jesus all men will finally be divided and judged by the answer which each has given to the Gospel first announced to Mary and then proclaimed to all who have ears to hear.

And what is the Gospel but this, that God loves every one of us? He loves us so much that He has given His only Son to be our Saviour. Long before we were even born God had already made that gracious decision about us in Jesus Christ. May our answer be that of Mary: "Be it unto me according to thy word."

CHAPTER IV

IMMANUEL

"Now the birth of Jesus Christ was on this wise: When his mother Mary had been betrothed to Joseph, before they came together she was found with child of the Holy Ghost. And Joseph her husband, being a righteous man, and not willing to make her a public example, was minded to put her away privily. But when he thought on these things, behold, an angel of the Lord appeared unto him in a dream, saying, Joseph, thou son of David, fear not to take unto thee Mary thy wife: for that which is conceived in her is of the Holy Ghost. And she shall bring forth a son; and thou shalt call his name Jesus; for it is he that shall save his people from their sins. Now all this is come to pass, that it might be fulfilled which was spoken by the Lord through the prophet saying, Behold, the virgin shall be with child, and shall bring forth a son, and they shall call his name Immanuel; which is, being interpreted, God with us; and Joseph arose from his sleep, and did as the angel of the Lord commanded him, and took unto him his wife; and knew her not till she had brought forth a son: and he called his name Jesus."

Matthew 1, 18-25.

"And I saw a new heaven and a new earth: for the first heaven and the first earth are passed away; and the sea is no more. And I saw the holy city, new Jerusalem, coming down out of heaven from God, made ready as a bride adorned for her husband. And I heard a great voice out of the throne saying, Behold, the tabernacle of God is with men, and he shall dwell with them, and they shall be his peoples, and God himself shall be with them, and be their God:

and he shall wipe away every tear from their eyes; and death shall be
no more; neither shall there be mourning, nor crying, nor pain, any
more: the first things are passed away. And he that sitteth on the
throne said, Behold, I make all things new. And he saith, Write: for
these words are faithful and true. And he said unto me, They are
come to pass. I am the Alpha and the Omega, the beginning and the
end. I will give unto him that is athirst of the fountain of the water
of life freely. He that overcometh shall inherit these things; and I
will be his God, and he shall be my son. But for the fearful, and the
unbelieving, and abominable, and murderers, and fornicators, and
sorcerers, and idolaters, and all liars, their part shall be in the lake
that burneth with fire and brimstone; which is the second death."

Revelation 21, 1-8.

*"Behold a virgin shall be with child, and shall bring forth a
son, and they shall call his name Immanuel, which being interpreted is, God with us."*   Matthew 1, 23.

What a sharp contrast there is between Christmas, with
its lovely carols about the birth of Jesus, and the tense life
of our vexed world! That is the baffling incongruity of
Christmas which we felt during the war, and which we
understand again today. It almost seems out of place to sing:
"Glory to God in the highest, and on earth peace, good-will
toward men"! But that contrast and that apparent incongruity
lie very close to the heart of Christmas, for it was into a world
engulfed in darkness and despair that the Son of God was
actually born. Indeed, the very coming of Jesus provoked it
into fearful savagery, as we see right away in the slaughter
of the innocent children of Bethlehem by the command of
Herod, who was determined to destroy the new-born King.
And yet that was but a portent of even more terrible things
to come. For seventy long, bitter years the storm-clouds
gathered in darkening intensity over Palestine, and then at
last they broke in all their fury upon the Jews, as Jesus
Himself had prophesied, when the streets of the Holy City
were drenched in blood and Jerusalem was ploughed up like

a field. It was right in the midst of those seventy years that Jesus was crucified with wicked hatred, Jesus who was born at Bethlehem to be the Prince of Peace.

What is there about the message of Christmas that makes it speak in such angelic beauty of peace and good-will and yet point straightaway to the frenzied tumult of Jerusalem and the agony of the Cross? What is it that links the *birth* of Christ with the *passion* of Christ, and that still makes the tender mercy of God manifested at Bethlehem like fire cast upon the earth?

It is the fact proclaimed by the name *Immanuel: God with us.* Let us try to understand that.

"*God with us*" means that in the birth of Jesus Christ God has given Himself wholly to us, in a love that is absolutely unstinting and infinitely lavish. It is God's utmost self-giving that stopped at nothing. God could do no more than come Himself into our humanity, and give Himself entirely to us—and that is exactly what He has done in Jesus. The sheer extent, the boundless range, of His act of love takes our breath away. "*God with us*" means that God Almighty insists on sharing His life with us. Far from abandoning us to the fate which we men deserve, God has identified Himself with us. Once and for all He has become one of us, bone of our bone and flesh of our flesh. God has committed Himself to us in such unrestrained love in the birth of Jesus, and in such a way that now He cannot abandon us any more than He can abandon Himself in Jesus Christ.

That is why the birth of Jesus was heralded with such sublime joy among men and angels, for now that God is with us, the whole situation in heaven and earth is entirely altered, and all things are made new. Now that God is actually with us and of us, everything else is assured. Whatever may happen in the future, God's purposes of love and fellowship and peace with man will all be fulfilled. If God is with us, there is nothing that can prevail against us. If God has given us His own Son in the birth of Jesus, then He has already given us everything, and there is nothing that He will withhold from us. No wonder that the whole host of heaven burst out in praise, as the good tidings were announced to the shepherds: "Glory to God in the highest, and on earth peace, good-will toward men." No wonder Simeon said, when he took the baby Jesus into his arms: "Now lettest thou thy servant depart in peace according to thy word, for mine eyes have seen thy salvation."

The peace of God was assured, but the peace of man with God was yet to be gained. This is where the gift of Christmas takes on a deeper meaning.

"*God with us*" means God with us sinners in our lost and bankrupt state. Where we have sold ourselves irretrievably into slavery and perdition and are hopelessly broken and damned, God has joined Himself to us. God has refused to let us go. He has insisted on making Himself one of us, and one with us, in order to make our lost cause His very own, and so to restore us to Himself in love. "*God with us*" means that God is *for us*; God is *on our side*; that He has come among us to shoulder our burden, and to rescue us from disaster and doom and to reinstate us as sons of the heavenly Father. That is the meaning of the whole life of Jesus from His birth to His death. It was God taking upon Himself our poor human life in all its wretchedness and need, God living out our human life from beginning to end, in order to redeem it. . . . Think of a son born into a family that has gone down in the world and restoring its fortunes, or of a son recovering the family business from bankruptcy and setting it upon a solid foundation. Those are poor analogies, but they may help us to understand the meaning of the birth of Jesus as the coming of the Son of God into our human family in order to make our lost cause His own and to save it from utter disaster.

Child in the manger,
Infant of Mary;
Outcast and stranger,
Lord of all!
Child who inherits
All our transgressions,
All our demerits
On Him fall.

Yes, it was on our behalf that Jesus, the Son of God, was born—not for His own sake, but for our sake. It was on our behalf that He humbled Himself to live the life of a human infant, to share our life to the full from its very origin. It was on our behalf that Jesus learned to pray at His mother's knee, on our behalf that He learned obedience both to His earthly parents and to His heavenly Father, not simply to show us the pattern of true sonship, but to restore our human life to perfect fellowship with our Father who is in Heaven. It was on our behalf that He was tempted in all points as we are. It was on our behalf that He involved Himself so fully in the life of His fellow-men, sharing with sinners their daily bread, and in the midst of it all offering to God a life of perfect obedience where they were disobedient. And it was on our behalf at last that He was obedient even unto death, and in our place that He meekly submitted to God's judgment where we are resentful and defiant. But God the Father raised Jesus from the dead, acknowledging Him as His beloved Son in whom He is well pleased, and accepting in His obedient life and death a sacrifice on our behalf.

Jesus lived a fully human life, but all through that human life it was God who was living it for our sakes that He might reconcile us to Himself and gather our frail human life into union with His divine life. The whole life of Jesus was the life of God with us sinners, God taking our place and doing for us what we could not do for ourselves, God laying hold of our rebellious will, making it His own and bending it back

from its disobedience to obedience, from its defiance to love.
And so we hear Jesus praying in Gethsemane, "Not my will,
but thine be done."

Let us think of what Christ had to suffer in order to do
that. Do we remember the parable He told about the man
who planted a vineyard and let it out to husbandmen, and
went into a far country? From time to time he sent his servants
back to the vineyard to receive some of the fruit that was due
to him, but they were all beaten or stoned or shamefully
handled and sent empty away. Then last of all the owner sent
His only son, His beloved son, saying, "They will reverence
my son", but when the husbandmen saw the son and heir
come to the vineyard, they became even more wicked, and
they took him and killed him and cast him out of the vineyard,
and took possession of it for themselves. When God is in the
far country the conflict between man and God does not seem
so sharp, but when God is with us, when the Son of God
comes into the midst of our human life, then the conflict
between God and man reaches its utmost intensity. That is
precisely what happened with the birth of Immanuel. With
the coming of the Son of God into our humanity, man's
enmity to God was provoked to its utmost intensity, but
Jesus Christ came in order to take that very conflict into His
own heart and to bear it in suffering in order to reconcile man
to God. He came to penetrate into the innermost life of
humanity, into the very heart of its blackest evil in order to
make human guilt and sorrow and suffering His own. In
pouring out His life upon man in utter compassion and love
for him, Jesus uncovered the enmity of sin in its terrible
depth in the human heart, and drew it out upon Himself
that He might bear it on His Spirit and on His body in holy
and awful atonement, and bear it all away for ever.

All that belongs to the meaning of Immanuel, *God with us*.
That is why it is only with eyes that have looked upon the

Cross that we can look upon the birth of the infant Jesus at Bethlehem and understand the boundless love of God in giving us His only Son to be our Saviour. Now we can understand why they called Him Jesus, for He had come to save His people from their sins. And now too we can really understand why He was born to be the Prince of Peace, for it is through the blood of Christ alone that we have peace with God.

It is because of this that we can really enjoy having *God with us*, and so enter fully into all the rapturous joys of Christmas, and know that when all the festivities are over the joy remains because the peace is eternal. There are some people for whom *Immanuel* can only bring anxious and disquieting thoughts at Christmas, for they have not found peace with God. But to those who have, *Immanuel* contains a prophecy of a day when Christmas will no longer be celebrated against the background of a harsh and troubled world, for there will be a new heaven and a new earth, such as John saw in his vision, when he heard a great voice out of heaven saying: "Behold the tabernacle of God is with men, and he will dwell with them, and they shall be his people, and God himself shall be with them and be their God. And God shall wipe away all tears from their eyes; and there shall be no more death, neither sorrow nor crying, neither shall there be any more pain; for the former things are passed away. And he that sat upon the throne," that is, Jesus, born to be King at Bethlehem, "said: 'Behold I make all things new'."

II

THE WORD OF THE GOSPEL

CHAPTER I

THE LAMB OF GOD

"And this is the witness of John, when the Jews sent unto him from Jerusalem priests and Levites to ask him, Who art thou? And he confessed, and denied not; and he confessed, I am not the Christ. And they asked him, What then? Art thou Elijah? And he saith, I am not. Art thou the prophet? And he answered, No. They said therefore unto him, Who art thou? that we may give an answer to them that sent us. What sayest thou of thyself? He said, I am the voice of one crying in the wilderness, Make straight the way of the Lord, as said Isaiah the prophet. And they had been sent from the Pharisees. And they asked him, and said unto him, Why then baptizest thou, if thou art not the Christ, neither Elijah, neither the prophet? John answered them, saying, I baptize with water: in the midst of you standeth one whom ye know not, even he that cometh after me, the latchet of whose shoe I am not worthy to unloose. These things were done in Bethany beyond Jordan, where John was baptizing.

"On the morrow he seeth Jesus coming unto him, and saith, Behold the Lamb of God, which taketh away the sin of the world! This is he of whom I said, After me cometh a man which is become before me: for he was before me. And I knew him not; but that he should be made manifest to Israel, for this cause came I baptizing with water. And John bare witness, saying, I have beheld the Spirit descending as a dove out of heaven; and it abode upon him. And I knew him not: but he that sent me to baptize with water, he said unto me, Upon whomsoever thou shalt see the Spirit descending, and abiding upon him, the same is he that baptizeth with the Holy Spirit. And I have seen, and have borne witness that this is the Son of God.

"Again on the morrow John was standing, and two of his disciples; and he looked upon Jesus as he walked, and saith, Behold the Lamb of God! And the two disciples heard him speak, and they followed Jesus. And Jesus turned, and beheld them following, and saith unto them, What seek ye? And they said unto him, Rabbi (which is to say, being interpreted, Master), where abidest thou? He saith unto them, Come, and ye shall see. They came therefore and saw where he abode; and they abode with him that day: it was about the tenth hour. One of the two that heard John speak, and followed him, was Andrew, Simon Peter's brother. He findeth first his own brother Simon, and saith unto him, We have found the Messiah (which is, being interpreted, Christ). He brought him unto Jesus. Jesus looked upon him, and said, Thou art Simon the son of John: thou shalt be called Cephas (which is by interpretation, Peter).

"On the morrow he was minded to go forth into Galilee, and he findeth Philip: and Jesus saith unto him, Follow me. Now Philip was from Bethsaida, of the city of Andrew and Peter. Philip findeth Nathanael, and saith unto him, We have found him, of whom Moses in the law, and the prophets, did write, Jesus of Nazareth, the Son of Joseph. And Nathanael said unto him, Can any good thing come out of Nazareth? Philip saith unto him, Come and see. Jesus saw Nathanael coming to him, and saith of him, Behold, an Israelite indeed, in whom there is no guile! Nathanael saith unto him, Whence knowest thou me? Jesus answered and said unto him, Before Philip called thee, when thou wast under the fig tree, I saw thee. Nathanael answered him, Rabbi, Thou art the Son of God; thou art King of Israel. Jesus answered and said unto him, Because I said to thee, I saw thee underneath the fig tree, believest thou? thou shalt see greater things than these. And he saith unto him, Verily, verily, I say unto you, Ye shall see the heaven opened, and the angels of God ascending and descending upon the Son of man." John 1, 19-51.

"Behold the Lamb of God who takes away the sin of the world." Those words were uttered right at the beginning of the New Testament Gospel. Their speaker was a man specially sent by God to prepare the way for the coming of the Redeemer, and to prepare a people for His coming. He was the last in line of the Old Testament prophets, but he was more than a prophet: he was the messenger of the New Covenant, the immediate forerunner of the Kingdom. Standing, as it were, with one foot in the Old Covenant and one foot in the New Covenant, he announced that the great dividing line of the ages had come, the great turning-point in which the people of the Lord were to be given a radically new orientation marked by mass-baptism and the preaching of the Baptist which pointed away from himself to the Lamb whom God had provided for the removal of a world's sin.

John the Baptist was a priest as well as a prophet, but he was more than a priest. He was not only concerned with the temple liturgy like his father Zacharias—as far as we know he never entered upon his priestly ministry in the Temple at all. He was sent by God to deal directly with the people and to prepare the way for the erection of the Temple in the lives of God's people when, cleansed at last through the blood of the Lamb of God, they would be filled with His Holy Spirit. God Himself would then tabernacle in their midst, and they would become the living Temple of God.

The work of John preaching repentance on the banks of the river Jordan and baptising multitudes in its waters recalls two important facts from the Old Testament, one from the sacred history of Israel, and one from its worship. It recalls the fact that when God redeemed His people out of the tyranny of Egypt and out of the house of bondage with the blood of the Passover Lamb, He brought them through the waters of the Red Sea and then through the waters of the Jordan into the promised land, into the Messianic country. But it also recalls the fact that in between the crossing of the Red Sea and the crossing of the Jordan God provided His people with a form of worship in which they were taught how to draw near to God, trusting only to His mercy and relying upon His divine provision for their cleansing and pardon through the blood of sacrifice.

All that is recalled for us by the Baptism of John: the Baptism of Israel in the exodus out of Egypt and in the entry into the promised land, and the consecration of Israel as the covenant-people of God in whose midst He is pleased to dwell and from whom He requires obedience and worship.

D

All that had come to be symbolically represented in the liturgical institutions and ceremonies of Israel, but when the priests and the people came to rely upon these religious ceremonies as if their performance could bring forgiveness and cleansing and win the favour of God, God sent His prophets to protest against them, and to demand obedience and repentance rather than ritual and religious observances. The liturgical worship of Israel was worthless by itself, for its only real meaning lay in pointing to the mighty acts of God for Israel in the past, and in bearing witness to God's promises for the future when He would bring about a new Exodus, and bring all His people into the Messianic Age. Then God would send His servant to be the Mediator of the New Covenant and through Him as the Lamb of God the iniquities of His people would be taken away, and they would be healed.

That is why John has been sent by God. He is not that chosen Servant of the Lord, nor is he the Christ, the anointed Messiah; he is simply the messenger sent on ahead, the voice of one crying to Israel, in the wilderness calling them to repent and be prepared to pass over into the Messianic Age, for at last the Kingdom of God is at hand, and already God's chosen Servant, who is to bear away the sin of the world, is in the midst—as yet unrecognised, but about to stand forth and begin His great work of judgment and mercy. The time for religious ceremonies in the temple is at an end. In the temple there was a great laver full of water where the priests were required to wash their bodies before offering the lamb in sacrifice upon the altar. The Temple was made for priests to do all that symbolically for the rest of the people, but now the time had come for the real thing, for all the people to be cleansed in heart and washed in body in preparation for sacrifice and atonement. There was certainly no room in the temple at Jerusalem for that to take place, and so John was sent by God to summon the people to come down with him to the river Jordan with all its historic importance and meaning—and the people answered the call, for they streamed down to the Jordan by tens of thousands. The great moment in history had arrived at last, when the Lamb God Himself had provided was about to come, for God was sending as His Servant His own Son to be the sacrifice for the sins of the world. That is why John sent such a stirring message to the whole nation, calling them to come down to the waters of Jordan to confess their sins and wash their bodies in water as a preparation for the sacrifice.

John was ruthless with the people, as he preached. His words were like flames of fire that searched out men's hearts, and the people responded in a great movement of repentance, of inward and outward cleansing. This was a radical repentance in which the whole person, body and soul, was involved. It was in the midst of that movement, six months after it had begun, right at its very peak, that Jesus was suddenly found among the crowds identifying Himself with sinners in Baptism. "There He is," said John, pointing to Jesus. "That's He. There's the Lamb of God who bears away the sin of the world."

The next day when John was with some of his disciples, they saw Jesus again. And again John pointed to Jesus and said, "Look, the Lamb of God!" Two of the disciples who heard John went after Jesus, and when He saw them following Him, He turned round and spoke to them. And so Andrew and his friend actually met Jesus, the Son of God, and spoke with Him. Jesus even took them home and they stayed with Him, and became His disciples. The next day Andrew went off to find his brother Simon Peter, and brought him to Jesus too, and then Nathanael came. Already Jesus had begun to choose out of the multitudes of those baptised with Him in the waters of the Jordan a small company of disciples whom He could build round Himself as the nucleus of the Messianic

Community, as the foundation of the Church, as the Apostles of the Gospel.

The Baptism of John and especially John's Baptism of Jesus are what the Evangelists call "the beginning of the Gospel". How much there is for us to think about even in that beginning! We cannot examine it all carefully here, but we take three things from the account recorded by St. John in this chapter and consider what they have to teach us about the beginning of the Gospel.

(1) *The Lamb of God who bears away the sin of the world.* What does that really mean? John was using the sacrificial language of the Old Testament cult in order to describe the work which Jesus was to accomplish as the Servant in obedience to God and on the Cross. In the ancient ritual a man would sometimes lay his hands on the head of a lamb and confess his sins, as if transferring his sin and guilt to the lamb, which was then sacrificed on his behalf. Of course, that was only a ceremony, and it could not really take away his sin, but God gave such ceremonies to the Jews to bear witness to His divine readiness not only to pardon but to provide for the poor sinner a means of obedient response to His pardoning love, and so in this way God sought to educate and prepare the Jews for the coming of Christ.

At last Jesus came as a sacrificial lamb, and we find Him among the crowds confessing their sins and being baptised unto repentance. Jesus had no sin to confess, but He was baptised too in order to take upon His own shoulders the sins of all men. From that moment on, the Gospels tell us, Jesus looked upon Himself as consecrated for His ministry as the Suffering Servant, and He pressed toward the Cross where, bearing the awful load of human sin, He gave His life in sacrifice for us all. No one will ever be able to explain fully just *how* the death of Jesus takes away our sin and guilt. That is a mystery as unfathomable as the love of God which pours itself out upon us although we are not in the least worthy of it, and a mystery as terrible as our own sin against God's love which Jesus has stooped to take upon His own heart, bearing it Himself in unspeakable suffering and anguish. Let us be content at the moment to consider the *fact* that through the obedient life and death of Jesus our sins are blotted out and we are reinstated as God's children, restored to Him as if we had not sinned, or as if we had of ourselves completely wiped away our sin. Through the death of Jesus Christ we are reconciled to God, and God has put all our sins behind His back, and promised to remember them no more. In the Cross God has judged our sins, negated them, and has put them away, so that they no longer exist before Him. He has forgotten them, and we are commanded to forget them as well, believing that God has completely blotted them out in the death of Christ, and draws near to us as our loving heavenly Father in order to gather us up in His arms and to lavish His love upon us. That is the very heart of the Christian faith: "the Lamb led to the slaughter . . . by whose stripes we are healed".

Every man at the bottom of his heart is desperate for the forgiveness of God. What he wants more than anything else is to be at peace with his Maker, but he knows that he is a guilty sinner before God. That was something that many of us learned in a new way during the war when as padres on the battle-fields we ministered to people who living face to face daily and hourly with eternity found themselves stripped bare of hypocrisy and pretence and who came to learn in the face of death what they really were and what they really needed and wanted. It was then that the chaplain could quite simply point away to Jesus the Lamb of God as the only One who can take our sin and not only give us peace with God but restore us to full communion in the very life of God.

What strange people we are! We know that we need to be

forgiven, for we are estranged from God by sin, and yet our very sin and shame make us afraid to meet with Jesus. A few years ago a friend told me about a young soldier who came back from the army suffering from venereal disease. He was deeply ashamed, and when he went back to his village home he hesitated about seeing his doctor. He knew that the kindly old man was his best friend, for he had known him ever since he was a child—but he was ashamed to go and tell him, because he was more than a doctor, who as a friend and a good man would have spoken kindly to him about his wrong. And so the young man tried to doctor himself, but instead of getting better he got worse, rotting away in his terrible disease. I do not know what eventually happened to him, but his desperate plight and shame and pride present to us a true picture of the human heart. We know that Jesus Christ is the Great Physician who alone can heal us by His forgiveness and blot out our guilt, we know that He loves us more than we can say—and yet we hesitate to go to Him for the pardon and peace and healing we need so desperately. Surely the Love of God who condescended in Jesus Christ to take our disease upon Himself in order to remove it and heal us, does not deserve from us avoidance of it. When God has poured out all His love upon us, and stooped to bear the whole burden of our sin and guilt, then to insist on bearing our sin ourselves because we are responsible for it is surely to sin against God's love supremely, for it is to tell Jesus that He need not have bothered to suffer and die for us on the Cross. His love bore all other sins, but can it bear the sin of scorning it? We must not forget that there is a "wrath of the Lamb", of the Lamb who bears the sin of the world. The measure of that wrath can only be the measure of the love of God poured out in Christ to take away our sin.

(2) *Personal encounter with Christ.* Immediately after John the Baptist spoke of Jesus as the Lamb of God who bears away

the sin of the world, two of John's disciples detached themselves from the crowd and went to look for Jesus. Before long they found Him, and He spoke with them. Surely the Evangelist has recorded that to teach us that it is not enough for some preacher like John the Baptist to point us to Jesus as the Lamb of God. There must be a personal encounter with Him, a real meeting between us and Jesus. That is still possible, for Jesus Christ did not only die for us; He rose again and is alive and waits for us to come to Him in order to be forgiven and healed.

Indeed that is the only way we can meet with Jesus Christ. When the Son of God came into the world He became a particular man, the Son of Mary, the cousin of John the Baptist, Jesus of Nazareth. That is the only way in which He could become Man, by becoming a Man among men. We can only know a man if we are introduced to him and meet him face to face; and we can only know about him from others who have met him and known him and then spoken to others about him. All knowledge of persons is derived from direct personal contact, and therefore has to be communicated directly from man to man and person to person.

When we know Jesus Christ today our knowledge is not different from that: it all derives from direct personal contact with Him and is based on personal witness about Him. We can have personal knowledge about Jesus Christ, but can we have direct personal encounter with Him and know Him personally for ourselves? Yes we can, and that is the perpetual miracle of the knowledge of Jesus Christ. But this direct personal knowledge of Jesus Christ comes when two things happen: when other people communicate to us a knowledge of Christ, and when at the same time He Himself alive comes to us, using their communication about Him as the means to reveal Himself directly and personally to us.

It may help us to recall the story of Samuel as a child in

the Old Testament. God spoke to him directly calling him by name, but Samuel was unable to recognise the voice of God or to distinguish it from the voice of man. He thought that it was Eli the aged priest who was calling him. Again and again it happened, until Eli realised that God must be speaking to the little boy. Then Eli told Samuel that God was speaking to him and told him how to respond, so that when God spoke to Samuel again he was able to recognise God's voice and receive God's Word directly and personally. It is worth remembering also that the message God gave to Samuel was meant for Eli, who had become too slack and careless to hear the voice of God for himself, so that God had to use the little Samuel to speak to him. That is how God always speaks to us, not directly out of the blue, as it were, not simply through the witness of others. It is when both these come together, the vertical Word of God from above, and the horizontal witness of others, that we know God and hear His Word personally and directly for ourselves.

So it is in the New Testament, as we see very clearly in the case of Saul of Tarsus. On the Damascus road the risen Jesus spoke to Saul directly but he was blinded by the light of the revelation, and only after Christ had spoken to him through Ananias one of His disciples did He communicate His word fully to Saul. Jesus spoke to Saul directly from above, but He also spoke to him indirectly through another man on earth, and it was when both these lines of communication came together that Saul's eyes were opened and he was baptised as a disciple of Christ.

That is the way in which we encounter Christ personally and directly. Because God has become man in one particular person in history, we can only know of Him through personal and historical contact with that person—our knowledge of God in Christ must be personally and historically communicated to us through a human chain of witnesses beginning with the recorded witness of the original disciples. But Jesus uses that historical witness to bring us to Him, and to convey Himself to us directly. In this very Gospel, for example, it is John who is speaking and bearing witness to Jesus, and I am expounding what John has said, not simply in the light of what I think he said but in the light of what I have learned together with others in the Church of the meaning of the Gospel. I am influenced in my witness by the witness of others in the history of the Church, so that as we meditate upon this passage and seek to listen to its message, we do that "with all saints," in the communion of the Spirit. But in that very communion it is Jesus Christ Himself alive, acutely and personally near, who speaks to us, and we hear and know Him face to face, invisibly as yet, but nonetheless directly and intimately. That is the perpetual miracle of the Gospel wherever it is preached. It is preached by very fallible human beings, but through their witness and in spite of their mistakes, Christ Himself comes and meets with sinners directly and enters into conversation with them just as He entered into conversation with these disciples at the very beginning of the Gospel.

Let us notice what happened as a result of that first conversation with Jesus. The very next day Andrew found Peter his brother and brought him to Jesus, and we know well what that meant for Peter and indeed for the whole world. Nathanael was also brought to Jesus and he believed in Him when he discovered that the Word of God which he heard in Jesus was the same as the Word which he heard while meditating upon the Old Testament revelation under his garden fig tree. These earliest of all the disciples began by being messengers of the Gospel to one another, but at the same time there were angelic messengers at work, for direct revelation of God was given to them as they talked with Jesus man to man, and talked to one another about Him.

This also the Gospel has to tell us, therefore: it is not enough that we should encounter Jesus personally for ourselves, meet and know Him and receive from Him all that He has to offer us; it is imperative that we go and find our brothers, our neighbours and our friends, and introduce them to Jesus as well, so that they may believe not because they have heard us speak about Him but because God uses our witness for His supernatural revelation, and as the means whereby there is direct personal encounter with the living Christ.

(3) *The place of Baptism in the Gospel.* John's Baptism in the waters of the Jordan was given in preparation for the coming of Christ, so that all who were baptised by him were baptised in the name of the Coming One. It was when Jesus Himself was baptised, and the Father spoke from heaven declaring Him to be His beloved Son, and poured out His Spirit upon Christ, that John's Baptism came to have a deeper significance. But it was only when Jesus Himself shed His Blood on the Cross that Baptism was given its fuller reality as a sacrament of cleansing in His Blood and of adoption through Christ into the family of God.

The disciples did not understand all that until much later— and certainly they did not understand it when they were baptised by John. They did not even know Jesus then, but after their Baptism Jesus gathered them round Him, walked with them, talked with them, and gradually revealed Himself to them, until the day came when they confessed that He was the Christ, the Son of the living God. It was only after that that Jesus began to teach them about the Cross.

Is it really any different with us? When we were children we were brought to Church and in the presence of God we were baptised with water, poured or sprinkled on our heads, to signify our cleansing in the Blood of Christ, to signify the fact that Christ had died for us as the Lamb of God and made us His own. By that sacramental act we were sealed for

Christ and He promised us His love and forgiveness. By that act we were acknowledged by God as His children, not for our own sakes, but for the sake of Christ His beloved Son, and He promised to send upon us the same Spirit He poured out upon His Son at His Baptism. Just as Jesus gathered His disciples around Him in the beginning of the Gospel and taught them, gradually revealing Himself to them, until they confessed Him with their mouth and believed on Him with their heart, so Jesus now gathers us round Him through the witness of our homes and through the teaching and preaching of the Gospel in the Church, revealing Himself to us gradually, and asking of us the love and devotion of our hearts, until we come to confess Him as our personal Saviour and learn to enter into conversation with Him ourselves. Then it is, as it was with the disciples, that He invites us to sit down with Him at the Holy Table and shares with us His own Body and Blood in Holy Communion.

But how do we stand these many years after our Baptism? The truth of our Baptism still remains, that Christ died for us and claims us for His own—but has that truth borne fruit in our adult life? Has the fact of our Baptism been gratefully acknowledged, and all it promised been thankfully received? Have we actually entered into the inheritance of grace bestowed upon us in Baptism, so that we are now in faith what we were baptised to be? The validity of our Baptism does not depend on the water poured upon us, but upon the Baptism with which Christ was baptised when He shed His blood for us on the Cross. But He requires from us an answer toward God, the answer of a conscience that knows itself to be sprinkled with the Blood of Christ. In other words, our Baptism into Christ and all that He has already done for us requires as its counterpart a personal acceptance of Jesus Christ as our Saviour.

The truth of our baptism remains, but let us not forget

that, as the Bible tells us, it is possible for us to turn the truth of God into a lie. No sin of ours can alter the fact that Christ died for us, or that He has sealed us for His own, but we can nevertheless twist the truth of our Baptism into a lie by rebelling against Jesus, by denying Him with a life that does not correspond to our Baptism.

James and John, the disciples of Jesus, were both baptised in the waters of the Jordan, as Jesus Himself had been. Then one day when Jesus was approaching the Cross, He asked them: "Are you able to drink of the cup that I drink of and to be baptised with the Baptism with which I am baptised?" They said they were able—but when it came to the point, and Jesus was taken away to be crucified, they forsook Him and fled.

It is to that same point that Christ brings us all, the parting of the ways, where either we cast in our lot with Jesus, unreservedly committing ourselves to Him at His Cross once and for all, or we forsake Him and run away from Him, afraid, it may be, of the cost of discipleship. Questions about our commitment to Christ are put directly to us by the Word of God as we meditate upon the Gospel, but above all it points us back again to the Lamb of God who died for us to take away our sin and to heal us. It was into His name, into His love and into His death that we were baptised; it is to Him we belong, and therefore Jesus claims us for Himself. John tells us that when the Son of God came into the world, He came unto His own and His own received Him not, but to as many as received Him He gave power to become the sons of God, even to them that believed on His name. When He comes again, He will come to His own, to those who have been baptised into Him, and all who believe He will gather together as sons and daughters of the heavenly Father.

CHAPTER II

THE NEW BIRTH

"Now when Jesus was in Jerusalem at the passover, during the feast, many believed on his name, beholding his signs which he did. But Jesus did not trust himself unto them, for that he knew all men, and because he needed not that any one should bear witness concerning man; for he himself knew what was in man. Now there was a man of the Pharisees named Nicodemus, a ruler of the Jews: the same came unto him by night, and said to him, Rabbi, we know that thou art a teacher come from God: for no man can do these signs that thou doest, except God be with him. Jesus answered and said unto him, Verily, verily, I say unto thee, Except a man be born anew, he cannot see the kingdom of God. Nicodemus saith unto him, How can a man be born when he is old? can he enter a second time into his mother's womb, and be born? Jesus answered, Verily, verily, I say unto thee, Except a man be born of water and the Spirit, he cannot enter into the kingdom of God. That which is born of the flesh is flesh; and that which is born of the Spirit is spirit. Marvel not that I said unto thee, Ye must be born anew. The wind bloweth where it listeth, and thou hearest the voice thereof, but knowest not whence it cometh, and whither it goeth: so is every one that is born of the Spirit. Nicodemus answered and said unto him, How can these things be? Jesus answered and said unto him, Art thou the teacher of Israel, and understandest not these things? Verily, verily, I say unto thee, We speak that we do know, and bear witness of that we have seen; and ye receive not our witness. If I told you earthly things, and ye believe not, how shall ye believe, if I tell you heavenly things? And no man hath ascended into heaven, but he that descended out of heaven, even the Son of Man, which is in heaven. And as Moses lifted up the serpent in the wilderness, even so must the Son of man be lifted up: that whosoever believeth may in him have eternal life."   John 2, 23 to 3, 15.

This is one of the great passages of the Gospel in which we are allowed to listen in to a private conversation between

Jesus and a deeply religious man. We shall misunderstand the whole passage unless we remember that Nicodemus was an exceptionally earnest and sincere man. All that we know of him, both in the New Testament and in the Jerusalem Talmud, points to the fact that he was one of the most honoured and respected men in Jerusalem. He was a Teacher of Israel and a wealthy Counsellor, and, if the Talmud can be trusted, one of the two officers in charge of the water-supply in Jerusalem for the religious ablutions of pilgrims when they came up to the city in their thousands for the festivals.

The account begins with the fact that it was the Passover season, and that many believed on the name of Christ as they saw the miraculous signs which He wrought among them. Nicodemus was no doubt fully engaged during the day, which perhaps explains why he sought Jesus out by night, although the reason for that may also be that he wanted to talk with Jesus frankly and in private. Nicodemus began the conversation by acknowledging that Jesus was a Teacher sent by God, for the signs which accompanied His teaching bore witness that God was with Him. Jesus broke in at once with a startling statement: "Except a man be born anew (or, from above) he cannot see the kingdom of God." Jesus spoke to him in language familiar to Nicodemus. He was a teacher in Israel and knew that in Judaism a Teacher was regarded as a spiritual father begetting disciples through his instruction in the Law, but Jesus was speaking of something much greater, of being born again from above by God's Spirit. Nicodemus was also a Pharisee, a member of the sect that was very strict in the use of baptismal ablutions to signify renewal and cleansing, and the sect most keen on making proselytes of Gentiles, and incorporating them into Israel through a rite of baptism so that they could begin their new life in Israel as "new-born children." That usually took place immediately before the Passover, so that they could keep the feast with the other Israelites. Nicodemus understood the language, but Jesus was using it in a new way. Jesus was a Teacher sent from God, and not like one of the Rabbis; and certainly He was no Pharisee, for He was not at all concerned with ritual ablutions and ceremonies, while the only baptism He acknowledged was that of John the Baptist. What Jesus was concerned to do was to teach the Word of God with power, and to make people whole again in body and soul. What then did Jesus mean? What kind of new birth was this which a person could not understand without experiencing it, so that until a man was born again from above he could not even *see* the Kingdom of God?

No doubt that puzzles us as well, but this is the truth of the Gospel to which we must listen here: the understanding of Jesus and new birth belong together; apart from this new birth there is neither enlightenment nor entry in the Kingdom of God. Let us consider what the Gospel has to teach us about this.

(1) "*Except a man be born from above he cannot see the kingdom of God.*"

There is no getting away from the fact that intellectually the Gospel of Jesus Christ is utterly bewildering—it is so different from what we naturally think, so astoundingly new that we hardly know where to begin with it. Martin Luther once said that when a man is face to face with the Gospel for the first time he is like a cow staring at a new gate. P. T. Forsyth used to say that no matter how simply the Gospel is proclaimed, there are always people who turn away and say, "Oh, it is too theological. I cannot understand it." Yet all the time the difficulty was not really an intellectual one, because the more childlike you are, the more easily you understand it. The difficulty is that the Gospel is so new and different that it contradicts our own notions and ideas, and cannot be grasped without repentance and change of mind.

Is that not why Jesus interrupted Nicodemus, for He knew what was going on in his heart, better even than Nicodemus himself? "You cannot understand these things, Nicodemus, if you try to interpret them in terms of what you think you know already. These are not natural and earthly things, but supernatural and heavenly things. They come from above, and therefore you cannot understand them from below, but only from above yourself. The only One who knows is the One from heaven, He who comes down from above. It is He who can tell you of these spiritual things, and if you are to understand them you must be born again, born from above." And then with solemn reiteration, in order to show Nicodemus that Jesus himself is this One who comes from above, Jesus said: "*Verily, verily I say unto you*, Except a man be born from above he cannot *see* the kingdom of God." If Nicodemus is to understand, he must listen to the Truth as it is communicated to him from above; he must enter inside the Kingdom and see it from its inner and heavenly side, and then he will really see, for it is only within the Kingdom that we can have the heavenly light shining upon us and enlightening the eyes of our understanding.

That is something that all the Gospels are interested in as they record the miracles of healing when through the touch of Jesus ears are made to hear and eyes are made to see. Beyond and above the physical fact, those miracles convey a spiritual truth. It is only through contact with Christ that our ears are opened to the Truth from above, and our eyes are enabled to discern spiritual things.

If a man is born blind, it is impossible to describe to him what red is like or blue or green. Only if in some wonderful way his sight could be given to him could he see, and even then he would have to learn how to see, like a little baby. That is why Jesus insists that even in understanding we need to be born again from above. We need a radical change of mind and heart before we can understand the great truths of the Christian faith or solve the many problems which the Gospel creates in our minds. Let us make no mistake: the Gospel does create difficulties, sometimes even by its sheer simplicity, as in the parables of Jesus, or in the miracles He wrought, which we are not prepared to take simply. But the Gospel creates difficulties because it cuts against the grain of our natural reason and offends us; it tells us that we are in error, and do not possess the Truth in ourselves, and we don't like it. It tells us that we can only know the Truth if we are prepared to deny ourselves, to acknowledge that we are in un-truth, and need to be put in the right with the Truth. It tells us in fact that the Truth is a living Person, that Jesus Christ is the Truth and only when we are reconciled to Him who is the Truth are we in a position to understand it. But this means that the hidden reasons of the heart by which we justify ourselves in our sin and barricade ourselves against the Truth have to be demolished, and the inner shape of our mind has to be radically altered through obedience to Christ. In fact, we must let the Truth of Christ get inside us if we are to see the Kingdom of God and grasp all that it tells us.

This does not mean that until a man is born again he must be entirely in the dark, and has to take some sort of blind leap into the Kingdom of God. On the contrary. Jesus always adapts Himself in His Gospel to our capacities, and He accommodates Himself to the amount of knowledge we may have. He always gives us enough to know to bring us to Him, so that in direct surrender to His Truth and Love we may be initiated into the Kingdom and be given to understand it from within. That is what Jesus called the mystery of the Kingdom. To those who are without He spoke in parables, simple direct homely comparisons by means of which He began to awaken their hearts and to turn their attention to Himself, and then if they were ready He would reveal to them the secret of the Cross and the way of salvation. But if a

E

man stops short when he first hears the Gospel and is offended at it, his heart becomes hardened, his eyes become blinded, and his mind becomes proud, and the proud mind can never understand the Gospel.

Listen to Jesus again talking to Nicodemus. "I know that this baffles your reason, Nicodemus, even if you are a Teacher in Israel. But truly, there are all sorts of problems that will baffle you, for you will never be able to understand the Kingdom by keeping at a distance from it or refusing humbly to enter into it. You must get inside before you can see and understand it all. But you understand enough, Nicodemus, to come to Me, as you have done. If you give me your heart and mind, and let me change them, then you will understand." Even a Teacher in Israel needs to be born again as a little child if he is to see the Kingdom. Although Jesus adapts Himself wonderfully to the educated and uneducated alike, and makes far greater demands on those whose minds have been trained than on those of little learning, the way into the Kingdom for rich and poor, for wise and simple, is alike: unless they are converted and become as little children, they cannot enter into the Kingdom.

(2) "*Except a man be born anew of water and of the Spirit, he cannot enter into the kingdom of God.*"

Nicodemus is still baffled and hesitant. "How can a man be born when he is old? Can he enter the second time into his mother's womb and be born? How is it possible for a man to begin again, to change his life radically and make a new start? Can he go back to the place where he began, to the very start of his life and be born again?" In answer Jesus does not deny that in some sense a man has to go back to the beginning, for he has to repent, his life has to be undone, but he certainly could not be born again of his mother. He says in reply: "Except a man be born from above of water and of the Spirit, he cannot enter into the kingdom of God." Actual entry into the Kingdom involves a birth of water and of the Spirit. Undoubtedly Jesus refers to baptism, but not only of water, and not just any baptism, but the unique baptism of the Spirit of which baptism in water is the outward sign and seal. In Christian Baptism the water signifies death and resurrection with Christ, a new birth that comes through death to sin and resurrection to life by the power of Christ's Spirit.

Jesus could not yet speak plainly about that to Nicodemus for the death and resurrection of Christ, in which we share in baptism, had not yet taken place. Clearly we do not have recorded by St. John the complete conversation between Jesus and Nicodemus, but from what he has recorded we can see that Jesus expounded to Nicodemus the meaning of the new birth, as far as he was able to take it in at this stage, by using the contrast between flesh and Spirit to show that this birth was from above, and by referring to the incident in the wilderness when the children of Israel were afflicted by a plague of serpents, and were healed of their bites by looking to the sign of a serpent which Moses fixed on a Cross erected in the midst of the camp. How else could Jesus speak about salvation through faith in the Cross before it had actually taken place? But John has recorded this story of Jesus and Nicodemus for us in the light of what we know of the birth and death and resurrection of Christ, and he means us in the Church to understand it in that light. So we can now understand what Jesus meant more fully than Nicodemus could at the time. "Except a man be born from above of water and of the Spirit, he cannot enter into the kingdom of God."

The new birth of the Spirit is not a carnal experience, but something quite different. "That which is born of the flesh is flesh and that which is born of the Spirit is spirit." There is, however, a way of "being born again" according to the flesh which is often needed, when our carnal and natural lives require healing. It is here that the psychiatrist, with his medical and psychological knowledge, can be one sent to us from God to heal the disorder of the heart and mind by probing into our past experiences, sometimes, it may be, even to the time when we were yet in the womb, in order to straighten out the entanglements of our life and to give us a new start. There is no doubt that we need this medical care and that there it can do a great deal for us, but that is very different from being born from above of the Spirit through being forgiven and cleansed from sin in our soul. The psychiatrist can help with our natural or "carnal" experiences, but he cannot by psychiatry bring us forgiveness or undo the sin of the past, so that we are restored in God's sight as new-born children. There is no way of retreating backwards along the road you have taken to find healing and forgiveness and salvation. There is no back-stair into the Kingdom of God.

Only Jesus Christ, the Great Physician, who died to break the power of guilt and to set us free, can bring us healing forgiveness. Through the power of the Cross He can penetrate back into the past along the line of the transgressions and sins that have left their indelible marks upon us and perverted the very roots of our being, and undo it all. But more than that, He can gather up again the time of our past life in His hands and restore the years that sin has devoured and use them for our healing and redemption; and even when we have wasted our life and it has perished down to the very ground, He can resurrect it again out of its grave of hopeless corruption and decay and renew it unto eternity.

This new life that Jesus Christ gives by the power of His death and resurrection cannot but have its impact upon our carnal and natural experiences from day to day, but it is as different from them as flesh is from Spirit; and cannot therefore be explained by tracing its antecedents in our past experiences. Some people think they can understand conversion by psychology, and explain it away by the embryonic processes of the heart and the mind. The new birth certainly does entail embryonic processes of the heart and mind, but it can never be explained that way, by its natural antecedents. Flesh is flesh, said Jesus, but Spirit is Spirit. The new birth is of Spiritual origin. It comes by a virgin birth in the soul from above nature, not by an evolution out of the old man, but by an act of God's Spirit breaking into our soul and opening it from above and bestowing upon us a new nature in Christ Jesus.

There is, therefore, nothing we can do in the flesh by which we can recover the child-like heart, for we are quite unable to alter our natures or give ourselves a new spirit. We cannot build a bridge from the natural life to the spiritual life; we are not free to constitute ourselves children of God or to grant ourselves forgiveness, or to resurrect ourselves out of the grave of the past and to begin all over again. We need to be born again from above by supernatural power, by a miracle of God's grace. But this is a very difficult thing for us to accept, namely, that as we had nothing to do with our natural birth, so we can have nothing to contribute to our spiritual birth. We can only be born again, by being begotten. It is only by the grace of God that we can become new persons.

That is precisely the point which offends us, as it was the trouble with Nicodemus. As a Pharisee, Nicodemus was a deeply religious man, like his contemporary Saul of Tarsus, who spent all his life in trying to fulfil the will of God and in obeying the commandments of His Law, and he too had come to rely upon his own goodness and righteousness. The disturbing thing was that before Jesus all that was called in question. If a man could not enter the Kingdom without being born again, then all his goodness and righteousness was of no avail. That was always the disconcerting thing about Jesus: no matter how religious a man was, no matter how good, His presence always discovered to him that at heart he was a sinner, no whit different from other men, but desperately in need of a change of heart and of a new nature. Again and again that discovery made the Pharisees terribly angry, for it meant that all their righteousness was only an outward façade while inside they were common sinners like the harlots and tax-gatherers they shunned. Indeed, in the words of Jesus Himself, they were like whitewashed sepulchres on the outside, while inside there was nothing but filthiness and dead men's bones. Those sharp words were spoken by Jesus to good men, to deeply religious men. Such a man too was Nicodemus, unable to change his own heart, a guilty sinner desperately in need of grace and forgiveness. He needed to be born again. The only way to be born again was to be born from above, and that was above him, and out of his reach.

Nicodemus, I believe, wanted to be born again from above, and, if the Talmud can be trusted here too, he did become a disciple of Jesus. But how many of his fellows resented the teaching of Jesus, just because the new life He brought meant that the old life had to be discarded, and that was too costly! It is just here that the answer of Jesus to Nicodemus is so relevant: "Except a man be born from above of water and of the Spirit, he cannot enter the kingdom of God." In other words, to enter the Kingdom we need to be baptised out of our old selves and inserted into a new life, or as Paul used to put it, we must put off the "old man" and put on the "new man" in Christ. There is no way back to God except through the crucifixion of Christ, in whom our old life is put to death, that out of it there may be resurrected a new creation; there is no way back into the Kingdom except by reconciliation, by atonement, except by repentance and self-denial, by renouncing our self-will and committing ourselves body and soul to Jesus Christ—but are we prepared to count the cost, to cast in our lot with Jesus Christ, cost what it may? Are we prepared to submit ourselves to the Great Physician whose grace cuts through our natural notions and desires and ambitions deep into our souls to expose our sin and pride, to uncover our insincerity and vaunted goodness, and so to reveal our desperate need to be forgiven and healed? Are we prepared to be crucified with Christ, that we may rise with Him, the First-born of the new creation? There can be no new birth except through the Cross.

It is as true of the spiritual life as of our natural life, that there is no human birth without pain. The other creatures of our world seem naturally better adapted to the ends for which they were made, with instinctive and vital resources apparently sufficient for all their activities. They bring forth their young easily and die without dread. But human beings are born through pain and usually outside help is needed. Man's life is not like that of other creatures—it is cursed with estrangement and sin and guilt. Unlike them, his life is not found in nature, but above nature, in God. But his living relation with God is broken, for he has become a rebel and has gone the way of his own self-will, in sin against God's love and a selfishness that ruins every love. And that has become "second nature" to him. He was not made that way, but now that is his nature, a nature which came from God but has turned away from God, a nature in which the whole inner direction of his being is now deflected from its true destiny, so that he loves darkness rather than light. He loves himself. That is why it pains and hurts to be born again, for man must be unmade and remade, be broken and recreated, be slain and made alive again. That is why the Gospel "offends" us, and why its operation is "against nature"—but it only offends us or is against us when we love darkness rather than the light and refuse to come into the light lest our deeds should be reproved. In other words, when the Gospel hurts, it is because God in His Grace wishes to give us a new nature that displaces the old nature, a new love that ousts self-love, a new righteousness which casts off even our natural goodness as filthy rags. It is precisely because God offers us new birth and new life that the old must pass away.

(3) *"Marvel not that I said unto thee, Ye must be born anew."* This is the third time that Jesus insists to Nicodemus that he must be born again from above. There is still more to be said about the new birth. "The wind bloweth where it listeth, and thou hearest the voice thereof, but knowest not whence it cometh, and whither it goeth: so is every one that is born of the Spirit." Jesus is still driving home to the Pharisee that this birth of which He is speaking is "from above", and it is a wondrous and incomprehensible act of the Spirit of God in the full freedom of His power. This is not an earthly thing but a heavenly thing. Certainly we must speak in earthly language of earthly things like baptism in water, for instance, but behind it all there is a heavenly reality, a heavenly secret. Then Jesus goes on to speak about that heavenly reality that lies behind the birth of water and the Spirit of which He has been speaking: the descent of the Son of Man from heaven, from above. In other words, John wants us to understand that behind all that Jesus has been saying there lies the fact of His own birth and incarnation. All that Jesus has said in fact about the new birth refers ultimately to His own birth. He is the One who is born of the Spirit from above. He is in fact the only-begotten Son of God, and it is in Him that our humanity which He took from us through the virgin Mary is born again out of the old Adam into the new. In other words, it is in Christ and through Christ only that we are born again. As John's Gospel has already said, to those who receive Him, Jesus Christ gives the power and the right to become children of God, even to those who believe in His Name, who are therefore born (like Jesus Himself) not of blood, nor of the will of the flesh, nor of the will of man, but of the will of God.

This is not very easy for us to understand today, because we have turned the new birth or conversion into a carnal experience of the soul, and have identified it with a psychological event in our lives. This makes it all the more imperative for us to listen carefully to Jesus here, and to look above and beyond our own historical or psychological experience and find the significance of our new birth in Christ Himself. Christ is the only one, strictly speaking, who is born of the Spirit from above, but He gives the right to all who receive and believe in Him or are baptised in His name to become sons of God—that is, not in their own name, but in Christ's Name. Christ Himself is the truth and reality of our new birth. It is in Christ that God now looks upon us; not upon us as we are in ourselves but as covered by the Name and adequacy of His only-begotten Son in whom He is well pleased. That applies not only to our sinful natures but to all that we are now in ourselves, so that we must learn to take refuge even from our experiences of conversion, or of new birth, in Christ and find in His birth and in His resurrection the truth and reality of ours.

When the Son of God came into this world He laid hold of our humanity which had gone astray and corrupted itself. He the Holy and Sinless One assumed our "flesh of sin" in order that He might heal it, and turn it back to God, and restore it to communion with Him. And that is what He did all through His life from His birth to His death, through His wonderful obedience and faithfulness to God He bent our perverted humanity back to the divine will. And so at last in the Garden of Gethsemane we hear Him praying in desperate agony: "Not my will but Thine be done"—not "my will", that is our human will which He laid hold of and brought back into perfect obedience to God on our behalf. In other words, in Jesus Christ, from His birth to His death and resurrection, there took place the great "conversion" of our humanity, and its destiny, back to God. In and through His birth of the virgin Mary, His perfectly obedient life, and in and through His death and resurrection, He came forth as the First-born of all creation, the First-born of the dead, but also the First-born of many brethren. Jesus Christ is the New Adam, the New Man, and it is through sharing in what He has done for us, and what He is for us, that we are given authority to be God's children and to be born again from above. We are invested with His Sonship and are accounted sons of God. And so He sends His Spirit in our hearts, and like Him we can also pray "Our Father", because we also are now sons of God. But we are sons of God, not on the ground of our own experience or natures but in Christ, and on the ground of what He has done for us and in us.

If we look into our own hearts and lives, we can see many changes which God has wrought in us by His Spirit, and they are certainly the effects of our new birth and new life in Christ, but they are not our new birth. If we look into our hearts and lives we see how corrupt they still are, how desperately wicked we are, and indeed the nearer we get to Christ the more sinful we feel and know ourselves to be. No, we cannot see our new birth by examining our spiritual experience psychologically, by looking within. We must learn to look away from ourselves to Jesus the Author and Finisher of our faith, for we are dead, as St. Paul says, and our life is hid with Christ in God.

This habit that modern people often have of thinking and speaking of the new birth as if it could be perceived in the soul and is something to be possessed in themselves is a great snare to many humble and earnest believers; it drives them to despair or turns them into hypocrites, for though they try to live up to "born-again and converted" lives, they know secretly how sinful they are, and that considered in their deepest selves they are not new creatures. That is not the way of Jesus but the way of the Pharisees. Just as it is not in ourselves that we have to seek our righteousness but in Christ, so it is not in ourselves that we have to seek our new birth but in Christ alone. The animal is made to have its life in its own carnal experience, but man is made to find his life in God and not in himself. The Christian who lives out of his own experience of new birth is a carnal Christian, and has not yet learned to know that new birth is from above, and is of the Spirit, and therefore that it cannot be discerned below but only discerned above in Christ.

Let us recall again that Nicodemus was a deeply religious man, but it was precisely to him that Jesus spoke so strongly of the need for new birth and birth from above. There was another Pharisee of whom we know much more than of Nicodemus, Saul of Tarsus, who had an outstanding conversion which changed his whole life and who, as born again and baptised in Christ, was known by a new name, Paul. But Paul never spoke of new birth or of conversion as a psychological experience; from beginning to end it was of "the new man in Christ" that he spoke, because it is in Christ that we are given to share in the new life of the new creation. It is in St. Paul that we find the perfect fulfilment of what Jesus Christ taught to Nicodemus, and it was St. Paul who said, "Be ye followers of me, as I am of Christ."

Marvel not that you must be born—*from above*.

CHAPTER III

THE HEALING WORD

"After the two days Jesus went forth from thence into Galilee. For Jesus himself testified, that a prophet hath no honour in his own country. So when he came into Galilee, the Galilaeans received him, having seen all the things that he did in Jerusalem at the feast: for they also went unto the feast. He came therefore again unto Cana of Galilee, where he made the water wine. And there was a certain nobleman, whose son was sick at Capernaum. When he heard that Jesus was come out of Judaea into Galilee, he went unto him, and besought him that he would come down, and heal his son; for he was at the point of death. Jesus therefore said unto him, Except ye see signs and wonders, ye will in no wise believe. The nobleman saith unto him, Sir, come down ere my child die. Jesus saith unto him, Go thy way; thy son liveth. The man believed the word that Jesus spake unto him, and he went his way. And as he was now going down, his servants met him, saying, that his son lived. So he inquired of them the hour when he began to amend. They said therefore unto him, Yesterday at the seventh hour the fever left him. So the father knew that it was at that hour in which Jesus said unto him, Thy son liveth: and himself believed, and his whole house. This is again the second sign that Jesus did, having come out of Judaea into Galilee."

John 4, 43-54.

The first public incident in the Galilaean ministry of Jesus, St. John tells us, was the miracle at the marriage in Cana in which Jesus turned the water into wine. In the earlier chapters of his Gospel St. John tells us that in the interval Jesus had gone with His disciples to Jerusalem for the feast of the Passover and records His cleansing of the temple, and the conversation with Nicodemus. On his way back Jesus passed through Samaria, and we have recorded his conversation with the woman of Samaria at the well of Jacob. Now Jesus is back in Galilee again, and apparently the first place He visits is Cana. Was it to see the young married couple whose wedding He and his mother had attended? We are not told, for the main interest of the Gospel record at this point is directed to something else. How was Jesus received in Galilee, the countryside in which He grew up, after the remarkable happenings in Jerusalem?

Two verses in this passage answer that question. (1) Jesus tells His disciples as they leave Samaria and turn their faces toward Galilee, "A prophet has no honour in his own country" (v.44). (2) St. John tells us, however: "Then when Jesus was come into Galilee, the Galilaeans received him, having seen all the things that he did at Jerusalem at the feast: for they also went to the feast" (v.45).

What is the meaning of these two verses? Was Jesus mistaken? Surely not. Jesus is never mistaken. The Galilaeans welcomed Jesus with open arms—as a miracle-worker, as a wonderful physician; but as a Prophet, as One who brings the Word of God, they would have nothing to do with Him.

That gives us a great deal for reflection, for there is something terribly disturbing in it. It is possible to welcome Jesus with open arms as a Helper in our need, as One who will meet our difficulties, and yet at the same time to refuse to listen to Jesus and to hear His Word, indeed to refuse to have Him as Saviour and Lord. St. John gives us a clear instance of that later in the sixth chapter in which we are told about the miraculous feeding of the multitude of five thousand men with five barley loaves and two fishes. The Galilaeans were immensely impressed with His power to provide bread, and while they said that He must be that prophet who was to come into the world, they wanted to take Jesus by force and make Him a king; they wanted to turn His wonderful powers to their own political and economic advantage. But when the day following Jesus taught some of them the meaning of the miracle, which did not lie in the actual food but in the Words that He spoke and through which He gave them heavenly bread for their souls, they were offended at Him. And when Jesus insisted that it was the Word made flesh in His own person that He had come to give them, and so give them to share in the heavenly and divine life, even many of His disciples left Him.

That is still true, desperately true. We are always ready to welcome the pastoral care of Jesus, His treatment of the sick

and the suffering, His feeding of the hungry, and His comfort
for the anxious and the distressed, as they are ministered to us
through the Church, but it is quite another attitude that we
are prone to adopt toward the Message of Christ, to the Word
of the Prophet, to the Gospel of the Saviour, and to the Sacrament in which we are given to eat His flesh and drink His
blood. We want all the material benefits of the Christian
faith, without the mighty Word of God at the heart of it,
from which all these other benefits flow.

That is the light in which St. John wants us to read his
record of the healing of the nobleman's son, for it is in this
story that we see how the Word made flesh in Jesus Christ is
received by men, and how He deals with them in His tender
mercy and healing power.

Away down yonder in Capernaum by the side of the Lake
there was an anxious home, and in that home a bedroom in
which a little child lay dying with fever. The family had
been unable to go to the feast at Jerusalem, for the little boy
was too ill to take and too ill to be left, and now he was
steadily getting worse. By the time the neighbours came back
from Jerusalem he was desperate. Some of them came to ask
how he was, and they spoke of the wonderful things that
Jesus had been doing in Jerusalem, miraculously healing
many people. And then news came that Jesus was at Cana,
only about thirty miles away up behind the Galilaean hills on
the road to Samaria. The father made up his mind quickly
and set off at once to find Jesus, in order to bring Him back
to Capernaum. He found Him still in Cana and he besought
Him to come down and heal his son for he was at the point
of death.

Jesus looked at the poor man distraught with anxiety and
desperately eager to get what he wanted. Was this another
typical Galilaean who wanted healing but did not want the
Word of God? Of course he wanted his dear son to be healed,

but did he also want salvation for himself and for all his family? And Jesus said unto him: "Except ye see signs and wonders ye will not believe." Jesus was well known in Galilee, and in Capernaum, but not as a wonderful Physician. Apparently no miracles of healing had yet been performed in Galilee.

The nobleman was insistent. "Lord, come down ere my child dies." That is the prayer of an anguished father, driven to his knees by desperate anxiety for his son. You can hear the very throb of his heart in his words. We all understand that well, for it is so true of us. When God touches the life of one of our little children, or of a loved one, we are driven to our knees in desperate agony, not because of the Word of God, not because of the Gospel of Jesus, not to agonise over the Bible, to eat its Words and drink its Gospel, but because a little child is at the point of death and it breaks our heart. Is there not that much of the Galilaean in us all? You can tell by the moments when your prayer-life is most sincere and tear-stained how true that may be.

But listen to what we are told in this passage. In spite of all that, we never go to Jesus in vain, no matter what our motives are in going to Him. His compassion is boundless. His love cannot resist such a father's agony. But there is an agony too at the heart of Jesus. It tears at His soul, it crucifies Him, to see that such hot passionate prayers come only when we are driven to our knees by illness or hurt or desperation. "Except ye see signs and wonders ye will not believe." Too much of our religion is altogether dependent on what we want to get out of it for ourselves.

What then does Jesus do for the poor man? He sends him away with only five or six words in his ear! "Go thy way; thy son liveth." That is all He does—He sends him off home with only a Word. The poor father had besought Jesus to come down to Capernaum, but Jesus does not go down. He does not even give him any medical advice. He sends him away with a bare Word, but it is the Word of a Prophet. It is the Word of the living God.

Jesus was putting this man to the test. He had not come up to Cana because he honoured Jesus as a Prophet, nor because he believed in Him as the Messiah or Saviour, but only because Jesus was a wonderful doctor. Besides, to have sent him away only with the fulfilment of his bare request would have given an entirely false impression of Jesus and His mission, and it would have left the man contented with only material blessings. Jesus deliberately refused to be a mere doctor. He refused to do what the man wanted Him to do, but He did give more than anything else. He gave Him his Word.

Will the father be content with the Word of Jesus? Will he return and take back the Word of Jesus to his heart and to his home? That is the crucial point in the story, the climax of the whole passage. "And the man believed the word that Jesus had spoken unto him, and went his way." It was the next day probably before he got back to Capernaum, but on the way he met his servants with the news that the child was alive and well. The fever had left him at the very moment when Jesus had spoken and the father had believed His bare Word, and turned to go home. He had a long way to go before he saw the fulfilment of the Word of Jesus, but when he did reach home he found that the Word of Jesus was indeed as he had believed it to be, the Word of Life. "And the man believed, and his whole house." That is the greatest miracle of all, and it also shows that the father did know before something of the real mission of Jesus, something of His messianic purpose and work, though hitherto he had paid no attention to it. What a home-coming that was! They looked for a physician, and they found the Saviour of the world. It makes a difference to the whole house when the father believes in Jesus and takes His Word back to his family.

What is the Word of God out of this evangelical record for us today? We are like this man from Capernaum, very much more than we realise. How dearly we would like to have Jesus come down to earth again, come down to our home, to make things right. But all we have is the Word of Jesus—no spectacular miracle, no scientific demonstration, no outward presence, only the Word. And we are asked to receive it and believe it. And here we have it in the Gospel of St. John, in this very story we have been reading, for in it we listen to the Word of Jesus speaking to us right out of the pages of the New Testament into our hearts.

But what is the Word of Jesus? It is Jesus Christ Himself, the Word made flesh, the living and the life-giving Word. It is Jesus Christ clothed with His deeds of kindness and mercy, clothed with His revelation of the Father, clothed with the Truth of God in the form of our humanity. It is Jesus Christ clothed with His own Gospel who comes to us through the Words of the Gospel offering Himself to us in and through them, as our Saviour and Lord, and also as our great Physician.

According to the will of Christ, and through the inspiration of His Holy Spirit, these Gospel records have been handed down to us, pregnant with light and meaning, earthen vessels to be sure, but containing and conveying to us heavenly treasure. These evangelical records have been committed to the Church to be handled as heavenly oracles so that the ministers of the Word of God in the Church are to dispense them as stewards of the mysteries of God. It belongs to their ministry to expound the Word of God in these Scriptures, and to put it into the ears of the congregation that they may receive it as the very Word of Christ and make it their own. And when they do that they discover that they have far more than a Word in their ear, they have Jesus Christ Himself in their midst.

What did Jesus first say to the nobleman? "Except ye see

F

signs and wonders ye will not believe." And He says the same to us also, but at the same time He has compassion on us and on our weakness. He knows how difficult it is for us, who do not see Him, who cannot touch and handle Him with our hands, and talk with Him face to face as we can with our neighbours, to take in and understand all that He would have us receive from Him. And so in His compassion He has graciously condescended to give us signs and wonders along with which and through which we may receive His Word, receive Himself the Word made flesh. These signs and wonders are the holy Sacraments which He has appointed to accompany the preaching of the Gospel as means to beget faith, to help our weakness, and actually to convey Himself to us so that we have living communion with Him, and with Him are raised up in fellowship and adoration to the face of our heavenly Father.

There are two kinds of signs and wonders, two kinds of miracles. There is the miracle which is a supernatural act clothed in a supernatural form; but there is also a supernatural act clothed in a natural form, and this is, if comparisons are to be drawn, the greater miracle. The first kind of miracle we see in the miraculous acts of healing recorded in the Gospels, such as this, in which beyond the power of man and beyond the power of any human science using even the wonderful gifts of God, God's creative Word is active upon His own creation, recreating it where it was blind, or deaf, or lame, or even dead. But the other kind of miracle we also see in the Gospels, in the sacraments of Baptism and the Lord's Supper. They are also signs and wonders, but in them God always makes use of natural forms such as water and bread and wine. They are no less supernatural, for it is God's creative Word that is at work in them, but at work upon us under the natural veil of water, bread and wine, in such a way that while water remains water, and bread and wine

remain bread and wine, even when consecrated to this holy
use, in and through them Jesus Christ crucified and risen
comes to us and communicates Himself to us with all His
saving power and grace, and blesses us with the gift of His
Holy Spirit.

But these signs are nothing in themselves. What matters is
not the natural elements of water, bread and wine, but the
living Word of God who offers Himself to us through the
promises of the Gospel to which the sacramental signs are
attached at the command of Christ as signs and seals that He
will actually fulfil what He promises. Apart from that Word,
and apart from its proclamation in the Gospel, the sacramental
signs are nothing but mere water, bread and wine. But when
they are used in this holy way as the gifts of Christ, as the
means through which Christ clothed in the words of the
Gospel comes to us, then they are the vessels that bring to us
the Bread of Life, the Food of Angels, the Medicine of
Immortality, the Powers of the Age to Come.

But the way in which we are commanded to use the
Sacraments makes very clear to us how we are to receive the
Word of the Gospel which they confirm and convey to us.
Our customs vary a little in different Churches. In some of
them, at Holy Communion, you kneel before the Holy
Table, and the minister puts the bread into your mouth, and
puts the cup to your lips, as He communicates to you the
promises of the Gospel, and you feed on Christ in His Word,
as surely as you eat the bread and drink the wine. In other
Churches, the bread and the cup of wine, are put into your
hands, by the hand of a minister or of another, and you take
it and eat it and drink it, and so feed on Christ, remembering
His promises declared to you in the sermon, and repeated to
you in the sacramental ordinance.

It is out of His great compassion that Christ has given to
us these sacraments as signs and wonders to help us in receiving

His Word, but it is exactly the same thing that happens when we hear and read the Word of God offered to us in the words of the Gospel. In the preaching and expounding of the Word, the minister puts the Word into our ear, and we receive it through the ear and feed on it in our soul. Then we receive the Word of God through the Audible Word of preaching. In the Sacraments we receive the Word of God through the Visible Words of Baptism and the Lord's Supper, but it is the same Word of God we receive in both, the Word who has come to us in the person of Jesus Christ our Saviour, for the Word that He speaks to us in all His words is Himself.

Let us lend our ears, therefore, to the words of the Gospel according to St. John about the healing of the nobleman's son, and receive into our soul the Word of the Great Physician by whose stripes we are healed and by whose wounds our sins are forgiven. The Word which we hear from Him is the Word of the Prophet, who not only promises but who always fulfils what He promises. Jesus Christ keeps His Word. He never fails.

CHAPTER IV

THE GOOD SHEPHERD

"Verily, verily, I say unto you, He that entereth not by the door into the fold of the sheep, but climbeth up some other way, the same is a thief and a robber. But he that entereth in by the door is the shepherd of the sheep. To him the porter openeth; and the sheep hear his voice: and he calleth his own sheep by name, and leadeth them out. When he hath put forth all his own, he goeth before them, and the sheep follow him: for they know his voice. And a stranger will they not follow, but will flee from him: for they know not the voice of strangers. This parable spake Jesus unto them: but they understood not what things they were which He spake unto them.

"Jesus therefore said unto them again, Verily, verily, I say unto you 'I am the door of the sheep. All that came before me are thieves and robbers: but the sheep did not hear them. I am the door: by me if any man enter in, he shall be saved, and shall go in and out, and find pasture. The thief cometh not, but that he may steal, and kill, and destroy: I came that they may have life, and may have it abundantly. I am the good shepherd: the good shepherd layeth down his life for the sheep. He that is a hireling, and not a shepherd, whose own the sheep are not, beholdeth the wolf coming, and leaveth the sheep, and fleeth, and the wolf snatcheth them and scattereth them: he fleeth because he is a hireling, and careth not for the sheep. I am the good shepherd; and I know mine own, and mine own know me, even as the Father knoweth me, and I know the Father; and I lay down my life for the sheep. And other sheep I have, which are not of this fold: them also I must bring, and they shall hear my voice; and they shall become one flock, one shepherd. Therefore doth my Father love me, because I lay down my life, that I may take it again. No one taketh it from me, but I lay it down of myself. I have power to lay it down, and I have power to take it again. This commandment received I from my Father.

"There arose a division again among the Jews because of these words. And many of them said, He hath a devil, and is mad; why hear ye him? Others said, These are not the sayings of one possessed with a devil. Can a devil open the eyes of the blind?

"And it was the feast of the dedication at Jerusalem: it was winter; and Jesus was walking in the temple in Solomon's porch. The Jews therefore came round about him, and said unto him, How long dost thou hold us in suspense? If thou art the Christ, tell us plainly. Jesus answered them, I told you, and ye believe not: the works that I do in my Father's name, these bear witness of me. But ye believe not, because ye are not of my sheep. My sheep hear my voice, and I know them, and they follow me: and I give unto them eternal life; and they shall never perish, and no one shall snatch them out of my hand. My Father, which hath given them unto me, is greater than all; and no one is able to snatch them out of the Father's hand. I and the Father are one. The Jews took up stones again to stone him."

John 10, 1-31.

It is rather astonishing that Jesus should have begun this beautiful parable of the Good Shepherd with a negative. "Verily, verily, I say unto you, He who enters not by the door into the sheepfold, but climbs up some other way, the same is a thief and a robber." But that is something we can understand very well today, for there are many people in our modern world who seek peace, security, bread and salvation some other way, not by way of Jesus Christ. According to this parable, they are thieves and robbers, for they try to secure by violence or to steal what we can truly have only through Jesus Christ.

It belongs to the very essence of the Gospel that in Jesus Christ God Himself has stepped into the midst of our daily life where we earn our daily bread and have our whole physical existence. In other words, God the Creator, who made us all by His Word and who sustains all things by His power and by His Spirit, has come amongst us as a Shepherd in the midst of His sheep in order to undertake direct pastoral care over us. Jesus Christ is the Creator and the Shepherd at the same time, not only the One who made us but the One who alone is able to sustain our daily life and to care for us in every conceivable circumstance. The Gospel does not tell us that God has made us and then sits apart letting us do what we like, wandering about like sheep without a shepherd; it tells us that God has come into the midst of our very existence to take direct charge over all our daily life, so that all that we need is to be provided through His hands with peace, security, bread, salvation. We are to take them day by day as gifts from the hands of Jesus Christ, and are not to snatch at them as if we wanted to possess them apart from Jesus Christ, for that would be to try to steal them from Him behind the back of God. He who eats his daily bread without giving thanks to God for it is a thief and can only eat stolen food; and he who imagines that our troubled world with all its anxiety about the daily provision of food and work and peace can be directed into the ways of prosperity and happiness, and into salvation for body and soul, apart from Jesus Christ, and who does what he can to bring about such prosperity and happiness apart from the shepherdly leading and care of Jesus Christ, is a robber. If the Son of God has really become bone of our bone and flesh of our flesh, then to ignore Him even in our physical needs and necessities, and to try to bring about a kingdom of welfare among men without Him, is sheer banditry. How can we elbow Jesus Christ violently out of the way and then think we can get all we want by climbing up some way of our own into the fold of plenty? It is the Gospel that tells us, "the same is a thief and a robber". There is no way and no door into that fold except by way of Jesus Christ.

All this is supremely true of our knowledge of God and of His ways. If God the Son has come into the midst of our humanity in Jesus and has once and for all taken upon Himself our human nature, then we cannot find God apart from Jesus Christ, and we cannot know Him except in the way in which He has come to reveal Himself in the Jesus of Bethlehem and Nazareth and Calvary. To do anything else would be like trying to steal the secrets of God behind His back, and to pretend that He has not become man after all. He who tries to find and know God in any other way is a thief and a robber. Jesus Christ alone is the way to the Father because He and the Father are one. "I am the door," says Jesus: "by me if any man will enter in, he shall be saved. I am the good shepherd." When we look into the face of Jesus Christ we see there the very face of God, and we know that we do not and cannot see that face anywhere else or in any other way. Only face to face with Jesus can we know and see God face to face; and only in the voice of Jesus can we hear and recognise the voice of God, for in Him the Word of God has become flesh and the Voice of God has become audible in our humanity.

There are many people who think they can know God

behind the back of Jesus Christ, in nature, for example. Certainly we do see the wonderful works of God in nature, for God has made our universe as a theatre of His glory. There is a great deal in nature, of course, that does not point to the glory of God. We cannot believe that God made evil and pain and cruelty; and nature is full of these, especially the nature of man. But it is most important to remember that nature is mute. It does not utter any voice, or talk to us. The voices that we hear in nature are not the voices that we hear out of it, but the voices we put into it. It is our own voice that we hear echoing in nature, but when we want another voice to speak to us, to comfort us or to strengthen us, nature fails us, for nature by itself is quite dumb.

If a man's conscience cries out against him because of some shameful deed, and his soul is in desperate need of forgiveness, he does not go to nature to get pardon. Who ever did a foul deed and then worshipped the beauties of a sunset in order to get forgiveness? No, nature is so completely mute that it can only echo back our own guilty conscience, and if we look for a word of pardon from nature, it will only mock us. But there are many who seek solace in nature, just because it cannot talk—because it cannot talk back to them and criticise them. That is why to worship God in nature is always to worship a dumb idol. To fly from the living God, the God who speaks to us, to the gods of nature is to fly from dialogue, to evade personal encounter, and to take refuge in an easy religion where there is no disturbing voice and no troublesome accusation, but also where there is no word of pardon or healing. To run away from the voice of God to the enjoyment of the beauties of nature, is to "turn the truth into a lie", for it is to make nature tell us that God is beautiful but voiceless, that He is only to be seen and enjoyed but that He does nothing and is not opposed to our sin. To worship God in nature means that we are afraid of the truth of God and seek "to hold it down in unrighteousness", as St. Paul put it; or as Jesus put it, it is to try to commit theft and robbery. It belongs therefore to the very essence of the Gospel that we cannot find a place in the fold of God by stealing it behind the back of Jesus Christ, in whom God meets us face to face, by running away from His voice and taking refuge in dumb nature.

That is the great negative fact that this parable sets before us, but now let us turn to its positive message. The prime thing Jesus has to say here is that His sheep hear His voice and they follow Him. The picture which the parable sets before us is not that of the shepherd in our country but of the shepherd in Palestine, who to this very day goes in front of his sheep to lead them, and does not drive them from behind. Jesus claims to be such a Shepherd. He calls His sheep by name; they know His voice and follow Him. That is one of the great distinguishing marks of Christians in the world: they hear the voice of Christ. They know it and are able to distinguish it from the voice of strangers. "A stranger will they not follow, but will flee from him: for they know not the voice of strangers." There are many other things that Jesus could have said about His true followers, but the supreme fact in His eyes is that they hear and recognise Him by His voice, and put their trust in Him.

When the Son of God came into our world He became a man among men so truly and fully that He was easily mistaken for a mere man. No one could tell the difference between Jesus and a carpenter or a mere rabbi, so far as His appearance was concerned. And because there was nothing at all special about His appearance, the Gospels tell us nothing about it. God did not come to manifest Himself first by demonstrating His glory and majesty in any outward way, but by speaking to us face to face in Jesus, the incarnate Voice of God.

We are not able to see Jesus as the disciples were. How dearly we would love to do that, but actually we have a great advantage over the disciples, for they had to learn that this Man was not simply man but the Son of the living God. We have their witness, and are predisposed by that witness to believe in Him. And yet we are just in the same situation as the disciples, even if we cannot see Jesus, for we may hear His voice and learn to know Him through His voice, as they did. The day will come when we shall see Him as He is, but until that great day arrives all we can hear is His voice. By listening to it, we learn to know and love Him, and then when we see Him we shall have confidence, for we know the Shepherd and He knows us. Jesus does not count that He knows us, until we know Him.

We must never be so flippant as to think we can make a "blind date" with God, and so need not bother about listening to His voice in Jesus Christ, and trying to know Him here and now. What will He say to us, when that date arrives, if we have not known Him? "I know you not. Ye are not my sheep. I know my sheep, and am known of mine. My sheep hear my voice."

That will be the decisive factor in the day of judgment: whether we know and love the voice of the Good Shepherd or not. How many there are who cannot distinguish the voice of Jesus from the voice of the stranger, the voice of the Saviour from the voice of the robber! Can we do that? Perhaps that disturbs us. We wonder whether we really know the voice, the authentic voice of the Shepherd for ourselves. But if we are disturbed and anxious, that is surely a sign that behind the human words that God uses to convey to us today the voice of Christ, and in spite of these human words, we do hear the voice of the Good Shepherd, and it disturbs us. It is not enough to be disturbed. We must listen to the voice, learn to recognise, and to know the Shepherd by His voice. We must know the person behind the voice, know Jesus Christ as our personal Saviour.

The next great distinguishing mark of the Christian is that he follows Jesus. "My sheep hear my voice and I know them and they follow me." True hearing and true following always go together. If we really hear the voice of Jesus we are bound to do something about it: we follow Him and are ready to go wherever He may lead us. Unconditioned obedience is the cost of discipleship, for the disciple is called to cast in his lot with Jesus and to follow Him wherever He may lead.

The twenty-third Psalm tells us where the Shepherd leads us: beside still waters and green pastures, and so it sets before us the picture of the Shepherd going on ahead and of the sheep following the sound of His voice. But the Shepherd also leads them into the valley of the dark shadow, and into many places where the sheep do not like to go—even into the valley of the shadow of death. But listen to His voice. "I give unto them eternal life; and they shall never perish. Neither shall any man snatch them out of my hand. My Father who gave them to me is greater than all; and no man is able to snatch them out of my Father's hand. I and my Father are one."

Let us take note of what the Good Shepherd does not promise. He assures us in all circumstances of His gracious presence and salvation, and of the gift of eternal life to us as we follow Him—but He does not promise us final security in this life; He does not promise us bread to the full, and rich clothing; nor does He promise us a peaceful and comfortable existence in the world according to our own standards. On the one hand, He says: "My sheep follow me. I lay down my life for the sheep." That was the problem that faced Peter after the resurrection of Jesus, when God brought again from the dead that great Shepherd of the sheep. Jesus had laid down His life for the sheep, but He wanted to make it clear to Peter that if he is to follow Him he must be prepared to be led where he will not like to go. Jesus asked Peter, if he loved Him, and when Peter protested his love, Jesus bade him feed the lambs and feed the sheep, even though to follow the Good Shepherd might mean that Peter would have to lay down his life also. There had been a day when Peter was free to go wherever he wanted, but now that was changed; he was bound to Jesus by His Voice and by his own love; the day would come when others would gird him and stretch out his hands—on a cross. The cost of discipleship!

On the other hand, the Good Shepherd promises to lead us beside still waters and into green pastures; He promises us a table in the presence of our enemies and a cup of gladness that flows over in its very fulness. It does not matter how great is the cost of discipleship, in affliction and persecution, in sacrifice and self-denial for Jesus' sake, the cup of joy is as full as ever, and the peace one that passes understanding. But this is to be found only in following Christ as the Shepherd, in letting Him lead us wherever He will, in leaving all earthly security behind us, following only the voice of the Shepherd. It will lead us, without doubt, far beyond ourselves, beyond our earthly roots and comforts, beyond our desires and ambitions, but there is no other way to the green pastures and still waters.

We have been thinking of the great distinguishing marks of the sheep of Christ. But what is the great distinguishing mark of the Good Shepherd? How do we distinguish Him from the hireling and the stranger? The Good Shepherd does not run away when the wolf comes. He will never desert us. He has promised to be with us always even to the end of the world, and if affliction and suffering come upon us, He will be with us in the midst of it all, as He was with those three cast into the fiery furnace. We have had such afflictions and such fiery furnaces in our own day right in the heart of Europe in which countless numbers have suffered for the sake of Christ and the

Gospel, as they did in the days of the Early Church—and it always remains true: Jesus Himself is present in the midst and His sheep hear His voice and follow unafraid. Let us not think for one minute that Jesus deserts those in Eastern Europe today who suffer for their faith, who are imprisoned, tortured and condemned because they insist on listening to the voice of the Good Shepherd and following him. And many of them, called to be shepherds and pastors of the flock, follow the Good Shepherd in laying down their lives, for they are not hirelings to flee when the wolf comes. But the Good Shepherd is with them, and will never leave them, and even in death no one is able to pluck them out of His hand. "The thief comes not, except to steal and destroy. But I am come that they might have life, and have it more abundantly."

That is the meaning of the still waters and green pastures in the ancient Psalm. Only faith in Jesus Christ will help us when the destroyer comes, when the wolf is at the door. The wolf will come to every door, for even though persecution and suffering may not come upon us as it comes upon others, we all have to meet the last enemy and suffer at the hands of death itself. There is no one who can help us in that lonely hour but Jesus, who Himself has tasted death for every man and who has made a way through death into everlasting life. By His sacrifice on the Cross He has made atonement for our guilt and shorn death of its bitter power. He has laid hold upon death and brought it under His sovereign command, so that for all those who follow Him He makes it the means of entry into the abundance of life in God. There is nothing, therefore, which can bring comfort, and strength, and peace, and everlasting security, to frail human beings in the hour of their death, except the voice of Jesus: "I am the door. By me if any man will enter in, he shall be saved, and shall go in and out and find pasture. I give unto them eternal life and they shall never perish, neither shall any man snatch them out of my hand." That voice is the rod and staff that comfort us, so that, come what may, nothing can shake the peace and confidence of those of whom Jesus says: "I know my sheep, and am known of mine."

We desperately need that certainty and assurance today when the whole world so familiar and apparently so well established is tumbling around us, for God seems to be shaking not the earth only but heaven itself. It is lack of steady, unshakeable certainty that upsets the balance of men's minds in our day, so that many are quite unable to face existence; far less are they able to face God. But not so, surely, with Christ's sheep. They know the voice of the Shepherd, and know that He will lead them through the darkest valley into eternal life.

Smite the shepherd, and the sheep are scattered to become the prey of the wolf. But here is a Shepherd who lays down His life for the sheep in order to deliver them from the wolf and gather them into one fold of salvation and life. It is in His death that He destroys the wolf, so that the blackest place on earth, where the Son of God is crucified, becomes the place where the blackest of evil is subdued by the love of God and made to minister to the redemption of the world. By the Cross all our evil is taken under the command of the sacrifice of Christ and made to work together for good to those who love Him, and who hear and follow the voice of the Good Shepherd, not only because by His death our sin and guilt are removed, but because He who died lives again, and is able to make the very grave of mankind to become the cradle of new and abundant life.

Jesus lives. He had power to lay down His life for the sheep, but He had power also to take it again. "Fear not, I am he who lives, who was dead, but behold I am alive for evermore, and I have the keys of death and hell." "Fear not, I am the resurrection and the life. He who believes in me,

though he were dead, yet shall he live." That voice of the
Good Shepherd is still to be heard in the world today, and
nowhere more loudly than at the grave of all our hopes. There
is nothing of greater importance in the world than that today.
Nothing that can happen tomorrow, no event of world-
shaking importance, is more important than the fact that the
Good Shepherd laid down His life for the sheep and that He
lives again and calls His sheep even now by name. Those
who are His sheep hear His voice; those who are not His
sheep do not hear. A line as sharp as a razor-edge runs between
them. Some men hear His voice, but others are deaf to it.
Even when Jesus spoke this parable, some understood not the
things which He said unto them. And so it is today. That
must ever be a strange uncanny mystery to the Christian
who knows and loves Jesus Christ. Why should anyone hear
the voice of the Good Shepherd and not understand or not
want to follow? Some hear His voice and believe; others hear
and do not understand because they refuse to believe. That
line of division among men is the only boundary line that
Christianity takes any serious notice of. Every other line of
division is relatively unimportant. It does not matter whether
we are Jews or Gentiles, men or women, employers or
employees, rich or poor, but it does matter whether we hear
the voice of the Good Shepherd and believe or not.

Jesus Himself has told us that when He the Son of Man
will come again in His glory, with all the holy angels with
Him, then He will sit upon the throne of His glory, and
before Him will be gathered all nations. Then He will
separate the people, one from another, as a shepherd divides
his sheep from the goats. The sheep He will set on His right
hand, but the goats on His left hand. There cannot be a
shadow of doubt about the fact that that final judgment will
be the judgment of His love and wisdom, and that it will be
an utterly just judgment, even though it means damnation

to some and salvation to others. But at that judgment people will be judged by the way they have acted toward Jesus during their earthly life, and it will be revealed whether they have listened to the voice of the Good Shepherd calling them or not, and whether they have followed the Good Shepherd where He wanted to lead them.

If we wish to know how and where the voice of the Good Shepherd can be heard today, we must go out in search for the sheep that is lost upon the mountains, for that is where He is to be heard, calling the lost wherever they may be. If we wish to know where to find Him in order to follow Him, we must go wherever there are the hungry and the thirsty, wherever there are strangers without a home, the sick and friendless, the naked and the imprisoned. He came not to call the righteous, but sinners to repentance; He came not for the whole, for they have no need of a physician. He came to heal the broken-hearted and the blind, to preach good news to the poor, deliverance to the captive, and liberty to the crushed and bruised. That is where Jesus is to be heard and that is where He is to be found. Unless we too have heard His voice there and followed Him in His seeking and saving of the lost, can it be said that we have really heard and followed the authentic voice of the Good Shepherd?

When the risen Jesus wanted to be sure of Peter, He asked him three times whether he loved Him. And three times He asked Peter to feed the lambs and sheep of His flock. It may be that as we have meditated upon the parable of the Good Shepherd we have heard again the voice of the Good Shepherd and heard Him also saying the same things to us as He said to Peter, because He wants to be sure that we know Him and love Him too. If we are out to seek the lost sheep of God, and to help them hear and recognise the voice of the Good Shepherd for themselves, is that not a sure testimony that we have really heard the voice of the Good Shepherd, and are following Him wherever He goes to seek and to save that which is lost? "My sheep hear my voice and I know them, and they follow me: and I give unto them eternal life; and they shall never perish, neither shall any man snatch them out of my hand."

III

THE FOUNDATION OF THE CHURCH

CHAPTER I

CHRIST IN THE MIDST OF
HIS CHURCH

"In that hour came the disciples unto Jesus, saying, Who then is greatest in the kingdom of heaven? And he called to him a little child, and set him in the midst of them, and said, Verily I say unto you, Except ye turn and become as little children, ye shall in no wise enter into the kingdom of heaven. Whosoever therefore shall humble himself as this little child, the same is the greatest in the kingdom of heaven. And whoso shall receive one such little child in my name receiveth me: but whoso shall cause one of these little ones which believe on me to stumble, it is profitable for him that a great millstone should be hanged about his neck, and that he should be sunk in the depth of the sea. Woe unto the world because of occasions of stumbling! for it must needs be that occasions come; but woe to that man through whom the occasion cometh! And if thy hand or thy foot causeth thee to stumble, cut it off, and cast it from thee: it is good for thee to enter into life maimed or halt, rather than having two hands or two feet to be cast into the eternal fire. And if thine eye causeth thee to stumble, pluck it out, and cast it from thee: it is good for thee to enter into life with one eye, rather than having two eyes to be cast into the hell of fire. See that ye despise not one of these little ones; for I say unto you, that in heaven their angels do always behold the face of my Father which is in heaven. How think ye? if any man have a hundred sheep, and one of them be gone astray, doth he not leave the ninety and nine, and go unto the mountains, and seek that which goeth astray? And if so be that he find it, verily I say unto you, he rejoiceth over it more than over the ninety and nine which have not gone astray. Even so it is not the will of your Father which is in heaven, that one of these little ones should perish.

"And if thy brother sin against thee, go, shew him his fault between thee and him alone: if he hear thee, thou hast gained thy brother. But if he hear thee not, take with thee one or two more, that at the mouth of two witnesses or three every word may be established. And if he refuse to hear them, tell it unto the church: and if he refuse to hear the church also, let him be unto thee as the Gentile and the publican. Verily, I say unto you, What things soever ye shall bind on earth shall be bound in heaven: and what things soever ye shall loose on earth shall be loosed in heaven. Again I say unto you, that if two of you shall agree on earth as touching anything that they shall ask, it shall be done for them of my Father which is in heaven. For where two or three are gathered together in my name, there am I in the midst of them. Then came Peter, and said unto him, Lord, how oft shall my brother sin against me, and I forgive him? until seven times? Jesus saith unto him, I say not unto thee, Until seven times; but, Until seventy times seven."

Matthew 18, 1-22.

"Where two or three are gathered together in my name, there am I in the midst of them." In St. Matthew's Gospel these words of Jesus belong to a whole group of His sayings which the Evangelist has brought together because of their supreme place in the founding of Christ's Church and in the ordering of its life and worship (Matt. 16, 13 to 20, 28). Among them we have the only recorded sayings in which Jesus definitely spoke of His Church, but among them too we have His teaching about the foundation of the Church, the mystery of the Cross and the transfigured Christ in the heart of it, the life of self-denial of its members bearing His Cross, His teaching about family life, marriage and divorce, and the place of little children within the Church, and His instructions about the life of reconciliation and prayer among His followers. That is the context in which we have recorded these words: "Where two or three are gathered together in my name, there am I in the midst of them." It is not surprising that from the earliest times this verse has been taken to be the shortest definition of the Church, gathering up into small compass all the teaching recorded in several chapters.

Let us look at these words in that light. What is it that makes a Christian Church? When we gather together for worship, sing our hymns and have our devotions, and make our offerings, all that is deeply significant and essential, but what is it that constitutes the very heart and substance of the Church? That question is answered by this saying of our Lord: "Where two or three are gathered together in my name, there *am I* in the midst of them." The very essence of the Church is found in that *I AM* of the living Lord Jesus Christ. Where He is actually present and worshipped, there you have the Christian Church. Where He is not present, you have a sham church.

What did Jesus mean by meeting in His Name? And how did the Early Church understand it?

"Name" is a very important expression in the Bible. It often refers to the mystery of the person. When we meet a person for the first time, we do not know who he is and what his name is until he tells us. But by giving us his name, he reveals his identity to us. It is like that with God's Name. When the Bible speaks about the Name of God it reveals to us God's inner mystery, His identity. It unveils His heart and mind, and makes known to us His redeeming love. When God tells us His own Name, He reveals Himself to us directly and confronts us with His own *I AM*, and gathers us into personal communion with Himself. God's name means, therefore, the personal unveiling of His own heart and mind and will, His self-revelation.

Right at the beginning of this section in St. Matthew's Gospel we are told that Jesus and the disciples withdrew themselves for a while from the crowds, to Caesarea Philippi, and there Jesus turned to the disciples one day and said: "What is my name? What is the name that people give me? Who am I?" The disciples told Him that some thought that He was Elijah come to life again and some that Prophet of whom Moses had spoken. Then Jesus said: "But what do you say? What name do you give me?" Immediately there came the answer from Peter: "Thou art the Christ, the Son of the living God." Jesus was overjoyed and knew that the divine revelation had broken into their hearts, for God the Father had revealed Himself to them in Him. Then Jesus made a most significant statement: "Upon this rock I will build my church; and the gates of hell shall not prevail against it." The essence of the Church is indeed the presence of Christ in the midst unveiling in Himself the heart of God's will and love, but the Church is founded on earth wherever men bear witness to the Name of Christ as the Son of the living God. It is established upon a rock when Peter and the disciples have the Name of Christ lodged in their hearts, and they are gathered into that Name as the very foundation of the Church on earth.

That is why in Church we still gather round the Word of God. It is there that we hear the voice of God in Christ speaking to us, revealing Himself to us, and answer Him with our devotion and bear witness to Him as Saviour and Lord. There Jesus Christ is pleased to be present and to establish His Church as upon a rock. That is what it means to meet *in the Name of Christ*: to meet in such a way as to listen to His Gospel and to surrender ourselves to His love. When we do that Jesus Christ is alive in the midst of us. These two things, then, belong together: *in the Name of Christ*, and *Christ present in the midst*, like two halves of a shell which make one whole. It is that two-fold reality which is the secret of the Church.

Because "*in the Name of Christ*" also means Christ's *I am in the midst of you*, "in the Name of Christ" describes that supernatural sphere where the living Lord, the Creator and Redeemer, is actively present on our behalf. That is why throughout the New Testament "in the Name of Christ" describes the sphere where miracles happen. It is in the Name of Christ that the sick are healed, the lame are made to walk, the deaf are made to hear, the blind are made to see, and even the dead are made to live again. "In the Name of Christ" describes the sphere where God in Christ is actually at work, redeeming, forgiving, healing and recreating His creatures. To be gathered in the Name of Christ is therefore to be gathered into a supernatural sphere of communion with God in which salvation and redemption and sanctification are in active operation; it is the sphere of the mighty acts of God in Christ here and now in the midst of history and in the midst of our human life on earth. It is the sphere of downright miracle, and of all the miracles that cluster round this supreme miracle, Jesus Christ alive in the midst, mighty to save.

There is still another thing that we must not forget: it is by Baptism that we are gathered in (or into) the Name of Christ. To be gathered into the Name of Christ is a solemn sacramental act in which the Name of Christ is put upon us, and we are incorporated into His Name, so that henceforth we live under His Name and are called by His Name, and everything we do is to be in this Name. That is how the Church is founded and how it grows, as we are gathered into Christ's Name, and are built up together into one Household of the Lord, living at one Table, eating one bread and drinking one cup. That is why this chapter in St. Matthew's Gospel speaks not only of the gathering of the lost sheep, and the reconciled brother, but also of little children, all into the one Name of Christ to form the House of Prayer where He is in the midst of us, and where we belong body and soul to Him.

Now we must think more specifically about the way in which Christ comes into the midst of us, for the New Testament has much to say about it. There are indeed three main ways in which it often speaks of Christ as coming into our midst, and it is when we think of these that we can understand more fully what our Lord means in His words which we are considering. Christ is present in our midst as *Christ for us*, *Christ in us*, and *Christ with us*.

(1) *Christ for us*

Christ comes into the midst of men by taking their place. That is why when Jesus came among men He died for them upon the Cross. He took our place, the Just for the unjust, bearing our sin and drinking the cup of suffering on our behalf in order to save us and to forgive us. When Jesus Christ the Holy Son of God came into the world He entered into our human existence from within, standing where we stand in subjection to law and judgment, ranging Himself among sinners, and sinless though He was wearing our humanity of sin, both that He might condemn sin in our flesh and that He might take our place before God. And so He stepped into the conflict between Holy God and disobedient man, between the covenant faithfulness of God and the unfaithfulness of man. Where man refused to live as God's creature in dependence on Him and rebelliously snatched at his independence, where he refused to admit that he was a sinner under judgment or to acknowledge that he could only live by God's grace, where he refused to admit God's righteous verdict upon him and so to cling only to God's mercy, wanting at least to co-operate with God in saving his life, Jesus stepped into the midst of man's existence, identifying Himself entirely with man, but doing the very opposite. He refused to live in independence, but lived on earth in entire dependence upon the heavenly Father, accepting the status of a creature under law, acknowledging God's righteous verdict upon sinful man and submitting to His judgment, and clinging only to His mercy and love. Where man was rebellious, Jesus stepped into his place, and yielded Himself in entire surrender to the will of God; where man was disobedient, He was obedient, and where man wished to save his life by keeping it, He gave His life away for man's sake that He might save his life. And so all through His life but chiefly in His death He entered into complete solidarity with sinful man that He the Holy One might take man's place before God, so that where we the unjust have to stand, Jesus Christ stood for us, the Just for the unjust; and in Him there took place, what ought to take place in us, the condemnation of sin in our flesh. He did not come to judge man or to condemn him, but He did come to take his place under judgment, and in so doing to gather man back into the life of God. Because it is God Himself who came in Jesus Christ to take man's place and man's status on Himself, man is not sheltered from God but exposed to the judgment of His love, and bound to Him by a bond of forgiveness forged in the death of the incarnate Son which, while it judges the sin, releases the sinner and reconciles him to God.

That is the way in which Jesus steps into the midst of our human life and all its estrangement and sin, in order to take our place—but that means that we can only follow Him as those whose place has already been taken by Christ. If He has taken our place, then we can only follow Him by letting Him take our place. He displaces us. That is why He said to Peter and the disciples immediately they learned the secret of His Name, "If any man will come after me, let him deny himself, and take up his cross, and follow me." To be a disciple of Christ, to be gathered into His Name, means that we have to deny ourselves and take up the cross in order to follow Him. He stood in our name before God, and we can only stand in His Name before God. Therefore we have to relinquish our own name, we have to give up the right to ourselves, and live in entire dependence upon Him, that is, live not in our own name but in the Name of Christ alone.

The Cross of Christ in which He took our place in self-sacrifice, has its counterpart in us in a cross of self-denial, in which we allow Him to displace us. That is why Christ comes into the midst when His *I AM* is lodged in our midst, and dislodges our *I am*, so that it is His Self who becomes our

Lord and not our own self. God can only enter our life as the crucified Son of God, and we can only have Him in self-denial, in repentance, in being crucified with Christ. And so St. Paul who knew the meaning of the Cross so well could say: "I am crucified with Christ: nevertheless I live; yet not I, but Christ liveth in me: and the life which I now live in the flesh I live by the faith of the Son of God, who loved me and gave himself for me."

One day when I was a student in Switzerland a brilliant young German undertaking research in medical science came to ask me about the claims of Jesus Christ. We had encountered one another in a University debate and he was deeply disturbed. We talked for hours about the Gospel and about these words of Jesus: "If any man will come after me, let him deny himself, and take up his cross, and follow me." I have never seen a man so desperate as he was over those words. Great drops of sweat were wrung out from his brow as he considered the claims of Christ, and then he said bluntly: "If I become a follower of Christ, I can no longer practise medicine in Germany. I can no longer have Goethe for my god. I cannot marry my fiancée, for she is a rabid Nazi." And so he put all his cards, as it were, upon the table, one by one, and I shuddered at the depth of the sacrifice that he was called on to make in order to deny himself. It was a real crucifixion. But Jesus had laid hold of him in His love, and he could do no other than take up his cross and follow his Lord. Not long after he emigrated to the Argentine, persuading his parents to go with him and leave all their wealth and patrimony behind in Berlin. That was the beginning of many hard years for them, but they have never regretted it. They deliberately lost themselves for the sake of Christ and the Gospel. That young man was called Paul, and like St. Paul he also could say: 'I am crucified with Christ: nevertheless I live; yet not I, but Christ liveth in me."

That is how Christ Jesus enters into the midst of a human life, by taking his place, by crossing out the selfish ego, by planting His own supreme love in its place. It is of such people that Jesus Christ still builds His Church all over the world. What kind of Church would it be if each of us entered it in his own name, each in his own selfishness, and each in his own significance? The Church of Christ is built upon the Cross, and only those can meet in it who gather in the Name of the Crucified, who allow the Saviour who died for them to take their place, so that they may live only in His Name who is Lord and Saviour.

(2) *Christ in us*

Jesus Christ is not content once to have died for us and to have taken our place on the Cross. He insists on lodging permanently within us, within each of us, and within us as a Church. How does that happen? It happens through His Word. The words of Christ are not just like our human words that are simply spoken into the air and fall upon the ear without doing anything. His words are indeed human, for the Son of God was made man, and now His Word comes to us through words of human speech, but they are more than our human words are. They are creative words, words which do something, words that act upon us and remake us, like the words which God spoke when He made us and all things out of nothing. But these words are even more than that, they are personal words which cannot be separated from the person who utters them. Our words are not like that, for when we speak we do not communicate our living persons in and with the words, but that is just what Christ does do. In fact, Christ wraps Himself up in His words and when His words enter our ear and our heart the living Christ Himself comes within, and acts creatively there. These are life-giving words creating personal communion, communicating a personal presence; they are words that germinate in the human heart and create room for Christ there, so that He takes up permanent lodging within us. It is as we allow the Word of the Gospel to saturate our minds and imaginations, to penetrate into our memories, and to master all our thinking, that Christ is born within us, that all that He is and has done becomes, as it were, imprinted upon us within, and becomes so truly and permanently the very centre of our being that we are transformed into His image and likeness, and even partake of His nature.

Jesus Christ comes into our midst as a Church when the Holy Scriptures are expounded in the midst, so that through them Christ is alive amongst us, communicating Himself, an audible Christ. In the Church it is the business of the minister to make the words of the Scripture audible and understandable in the language of the day. Then the miracle happens; through the foolishness of preaching, Christ comes in all His saving power into the midst of those gathered in His Name, and He constitutes them the Temple of His Spirit, the Church of Christ. But each one of us should be a temple of Christ in which His Spirit dwells. Each of us should also be our own preacher, so to speak, as we receive the Word of Christ and meditate upon it and give it constant lodging in our soul. Then the miracle happens with each of us: Christ alive within. There is no other way for that to happen than through the Word, no other way to have Christ abiding in us than through hearing His Word or, as it were, eating it and feeding upon it until it becomes assimilated to us. "If a man love me," Jesus said, "he will keep my word: and my Father will love him, and we will come unto him, and make our abode with him."

Recall that beautiful Old Testament story of the farmer's wife who watched Elisha the man of God passing her house continually as he went on his rounds between Gilgal and

Carmel. One day she suggested to her husband that they should build an extension on to their house and make a room for the man of God, a prophet's chamber, and make it habitable, so that whenever he came he could turn aside and lodge there, and teach them the Word of God. Her husband agreed, and in due course Elisha came to lodge with them and to teach them. What a profound experience of God's power was their reward!

Is that not the way for us to have Christ within us, not as a passing prophet but as a permanent lodger? The only way to have that is to make room in our life for converse with the Word of God, for study of the Holy Scriptures that through their words which Christ has elected and formed for this very purpose He Himself may be found within us. On the other hand, the Church that does not give full place to God's Word, both in hearing and in teaching, will soon find that Christ has been driven out of His Temple by the traditions of men. The Word of God is always the primary means through which Christ resides in the midst of His Church, for it is through the Word that He personally holds communion with His own, it is through the Word that He strengthens and guides His Church, and it is by the Word preached that He rules over the nations as with the sceptre of His Kingly power. It is through this Word now that the Kingdom of Christ is at work in all nations and in all parts of the earth.

(3) *Christ with us*

Almost the last words of Jesus to His disciples were these: "Go ye into all the world, and preach the Gospel, and lo, I am with you always, unto the end of the world." That is His promise, to give us His companion-presence, so that wherever we may go or whatever we may do in His service He will be with us. Recall how in the Old Testament the presence of God descended upon the children of Israel, tabernacled with them, and accompanied them during their wanderings in the desert, betokened by the pillar of cloud by day and the pillar of fire by night. In every time of trouble they could take refuge under the wings of the Most High, and find that His presence was a protection to the believing and destruction to the avenger. Now in the Christian Church it is no longer any fiery presence full of terrifying mystery that accompanies us, but the gracious presence of the risen Jesus.

Even the presence of Christ can become strange and haunting. One evening I found a man sitting near me in a hotel restaurant, looking abjectly miserable and worried. I spoke to him, and this was the tale he told me. Long ago during the First World War in which he had served as a sailor his ship had been torpedoed off the coast of Africa. When they got into the boats, it was found that in his boat there was one too many, and they began to cast lots to see who should go overboard so that the rest, if possible, should be saved. But a young lad of only sixteen or seventeen years stood up and said: "I have no father and no mother, but Jesus Christ died for me, and I will gladly die for you." Before anyone could do anything the lad was over and gone. For years the picture of that act of self-sacrifice had haunted this old sailor and behind it all the figure of the crucified Son of God who had died for us all, but for just as long he had resisted the claims of the Christ who haunted his memories. He tried to drive away the vision by drink, but the more he drank, the more he was unable to shake off the haunting presence of the Crucified. Now he was aged, but Jesus Christ was to him only a presence that haunted him, not the gracious presence of an accepted Saviour or an acknowledged Master.

Sometimes there walks into your company a man of great presence, and immediately you know that there is something about him that makes him tower over his fellows. Wherever he goes his presence makes itself felt even before he has opened his mouth. But he that is least in the Kingdom of God is greater than that, for he may be possessed of a presence that is incomparable: the presence of the risen Lord. We all know humble people like that who seem inhabited by the power of the resurrection. It is none other than Christ Himself encountering us in them. These are they who through meditation on the Word and through prayer have long lived close to the Lord, and even their failings cannot obscure the fact of His presence with them.

But all this is much more true of the Church, of those who are gathered into the Name of Christ and who share together the fellowship of the mystery of Christ. Many come to that fellowship bringing the companion-presence of Christ with them. And as they come, their presences, so to speak, merge together, and in a wonderful way the living Christ is in the midst of His worshipping people, unseen but very real. Is that what people sometimes call "atmosphere", of which they are so sensitive when they visit a strange church, either because of its absence or because of the power of its presence? Certainly when the members of a church gather in their own name and in their own significance, and not in the name and significance of Christ, the fellowship is dead, and the preaching of the Gospel appears to bounce against a stone wall. But there is something much profounder than this in the presence of Christ with His Church.

On Easter evening when the disciples were gathered together in the name of Christ in the upper room after their despair, defeat and bewilderment, He Himself came into their midst, and said "Peace be unto you", and breathed upon them the Holy Spirit. Is that not what takes place above all at Holy Communion, when, as it were, through the broken bread and the poured out wine, we put our fingers in the wounds of Jesus and find that He is really and truly present with us? It is there above all that Christ comes into

H

the midst, for there the Gospel is communicated to us not in word only but in action, and in the real presence of the Redeemer: *Christ for us*, as we break bread and drink wine, the body and blood of the Saviour who died on our behalf; *Christ in us*, as we feed upon the Bread of Life and become incorporated into the Body of Christ; *Christ with us*, as we rise from the Table and go to our homes, knowing that we carry from the blessed communion in the Name of Christ the power of the resurrection and the peace of God in our hearts.

We must now ask: Why did Jesus say, "Where two or three are gathered together in my name . . .", and not "where one or two are gathered together in my name . . ."? That is indeed a great question to which many answers can be given, but here we must content ourselves with two of the chief reasons. *First*, the presence of Christ does not belong to one person only but to all, and therefore by its very nature we cannot have it except in such a way that we share it with others. Jesus Christ did not die for me only, but for all men, and therefore I cannot receive the fruit of His death without at the same time being bound to all for whom He died. If I try to keep His forgiveness to myself alone, then it is not His forgiveness that I am concerned with, but with myself. If I try to enjoy His presence alone by myself, then I cut myself off from His presence which is not given except to the whole Church. The presence of Christ crucified and risen is essentially a communion in which many share, so that I can only share in the communion while having communion with others in Christ.

Secondly, the Word through which Christ comes into the midst and abides with us is not a Word that I can tell to myself but something that another person has to communicate to me. In the Incarnation the Word of God became man, a single historical human being, and now that Word can only be communicated historically from mouth to mouth, from person to person. That is part of the incarnate nature of God's Word in Jesus that it has taken human form, and is therefore to be communicated personally and historically from man to man. And so God uses other people to communicate the Gospel to me, and it is through other people that His Word is addressed to me, and through their communication and through their words it is Christ Himself the Word of God who comes to me. We can, of course read the Bible for ourselves, and hear the Word of God in it for ourselves, but almost inevitably we assimilate it to a monologue with ourselves. Only if private reading of God's Word is corrected and nourished by hearing God's Word together in Church can we really hear the Word of God alone, instead of secretly displacing God's Word by our own desires and ideas.

And so Jesus promises that where at least two or three are gathered in His name, there He will be in their midst, to reveal Himself, to communicate Himself to them, and to gather them together by sharing with them His own divine life and love. We are all members of one another in the Body of Christ and each member needs the other members, just as he needs above all the Head of the Body who is Christ. God has created us in such a way that He has planted the solitary in families. So in the Church or the Family of Christ He saves us in such a way that He plants us in fellowship with one another, and to deny that fellowship or to withdraw from it is to cut at the very root of our salvation.

That was surely one of the supreme lessons St. Thomas learned during those eight days after Easter. He alone of the eleven disciples had been absent on Easter evening when Jesus came and revealed Himself to them, and Jesus did not reveal Himself to Thomas so long as he was apart from the others in his private corner. It was only when Thomas came back to the upper room and gathered together with the other disciples that Jesus came and revealed Himself to him, i.e. to him in fellowship with the others. That precisely is what He meant and what He still promises to do for us in these words: "Where two or three are gathered together in my name, there am I in the midst of them."

CHAPTER II

THE VIOLENCE OF THE KINGDOM

"Now when John heard in the prison the works of the Christ, he sent by his disciples, and said unto him, Art thou he that cometh, or look we for another? And Jesus answered and said unto them, Go your way and tell John the things which ye do hear and see: the blind receive their sight, and the lame walk, the lepers are cleansed, and the deaf hear, and the dead are raised up, and the poor have good tidings preached to them. And blessed is he, whosoever shall find none occasion of stumbling in me. And as these went their way, Jesus began to say unto the multitudes concerning John, What went ye out into the wilderness to behold? a reed shaken with the wind? But what went ye out for to see? a man clothed in soft raiment? Behold, they that wear soft raiment are in kings' houses. But wherefore went ye out? to see a prophet? Yea, I say unto you, and much more than a prophet. This is he, of whom it is written, Behold, I send my messenger before thy face, Who shall prepare thy way before thee. Verily I say unto you, Among them that are born of women there hath not arisen a greater than John the Baptist: yet he that is but little in the kingdom of heaven is greater than he. And from the days of John the Baptist until now the kingdom of heaven suffereth violence, and men of violence take it by force. For all the prophets and the law prophesied until John. And if ye are willing to receive it, this is Elijah, which is to come. He that hath ears to hear, let him hear. But whereunto shall I liken this generation? It is like unto children sitting in the marketplaces, which call unto their fellows, and say, We piped unto you, and ye did not dance; we wailed, and ye did not mourn. For John came neither eating nor drinking, and they say, He hath a devil. The Son of man came eating and drinking, and they say, Behold, a gluttonous man, and a winebibber, a friend of publicans and sinners! And wisdom is justified by her works."   Matthew 11, 2-19.

"From the days of John the Baptist until now the kingdom of heaven suffereth violence, and men of violence take it by force." What did Jesus mean by "suffers violence"? How are we to translate the expression of the Evangelist—in the active or in the passive tense? Professor William Manson of Edinburgh prefers the active tense, and translates it thus: "The Kingdom of Heaven presses in and men of determined purpose lay impatient hands upon it." The Kingdom exerts its way by force, storms its way in. Of the two alternatives that seems to be the better, undoubtedly, and yet there is much to be said for the rendering of the Authorised Version and Revised Version—the Kingdom of Heaven is under attack, it suffers violence. I cannot help but feel that both are right. In the Word and the Person of Jesus God's Kingdom storms its way in, but how is that done? By the Cross, by the passion of Jesus, for the Cross is the Kingdom suffering violence; it is the weakness of God, but the weakness of God is stronger than men. It is by the Cross that the Kingdom of God storms its way into the hearts of men and nations, and so the preaching of the Cross, of the suffering of Jesus, is the power of God.

What does Jesus have to say about that in this context? "*From the days of John the Baptist until now* the kingdom of heaven suffereth violence, and men of violence take it by force."

John the Baptist, said Jesus, was the Elijah of the New Testament, and to understand him, therefore, we must think for a moment of Elijah.

The supreme thing about Elijah was that he was not only a prophet, but more than a prophet. He was a man of action. He did not just proclaim the Word of God, and say: "Thus saith the Lord . . . there you are. Take it or leave it." Elijah confronted people with God's Word in such a way as to force them to make up their minds one way or the other. That is the story of his controversy with the people of Israel, which reached its climax in the events on Mount Carmel. Elijah manœuvred the situation in such a way that the whole nation, King and all, were forced to decide for the Lord or for Baal, for God or against God. "How long halt ye between two opinions? If God be God then worship God." It was the most dramatic moment in history for centuries.

But after Carmel, what do we see? Elijah under the Juniper tree, utterly cast down and disillusioned. Why had not God acted? Why did He not complete the work begun on Carmel? Why was Jezebel still in power and allowed to go on flouting the living God?

Elijah had misunderstood the violence of God. And God had to teach him on Mount Horeb. What violence was there! A mighty wind rent the mountains and broke the rocks in pieces, and after the wind an earthquake, and after the earthquake a fire—but God was not in the wind, nor in the earthquake, nor in the fire. After the fire there was a still small Voice. That was the violence of God.

Elijah's part was to mediate the Word of God and to force the people to come to a decision—that is why Ahab called him "the troubler of Israel". But the violence of the Kingdom in all that was the still small Voice, and it was mightier by far than all the pent-up forces of nature unleashed in their fury.

Now come to the New Testament. For centuries and centuries the prophets of the Old Testament had proclaimed the Law and Word of God. They had preached about the coming of the Kingdom in all its power. But at last comes God's messenger, incontrovertibly the greatest figure that had appeared on earth for hundreds of years, an Elijah of a man—John the Baptist.

For thirty years he had fasted and prayed in the desert until the fire of God ate him up and the thunder of God lived in his voice. Then one day he appeared on the banks of the Jordan and preached: "Repent, for the Kingdom of God is at hand!" He preached in such a way and preached such a message that the whole of Judaea and Galilee trekked out to listen to him. This time the dramatic setting is not laid on Mount Carmel, but on the banks of the river Jordan, where John preached in such a way as to force people to make up their minds in the waters of Baptism. This is not the easy-going take-it-or-leave-it preaching of men in soft raiment, but the most forceful and compelling preaching Israel had ever heard, until they fell down on their knees by the tens of thousands, confessed their sins and went down into the waters of Jordan to be baptised in the name of the coming Messiah. At last the Kingdom seemed to be storming its way into the hearts of Israel, and at that very moment the Messiah Himself came upon the scene, the King of the Kingdom of God—Jesus Himself.

Then what do we see? Elijah is again under his Juniper tree. John the Baptist languishes in prison. His fiery denunciations had brought upon his head the wrath of Herod and Herodias, the Ahab and Jezebel of the New Testament. But it is not prison that worries John the Baptist, it is something else. In his great prophetic visions John had seen a mighty Messiah, one with an upraised axe with which He was ready to fell a tree at a single blow. He saw the Messiah with a threshing-flail in his hand, as he gathered the grain and cast the chaff into the fire. And now, what does he see in Jesus? A simple sower who passes quietly by casting his seed into the soil. A kindly physician who heals the sick and cares for the poor and needy. Surely this Jesus could not be the mighty Son of God, the promised Deliverer of Israel? Jesus seemed to lack the most decisive characteristics of John's expectations

—the Spirit that would rend the mountains and break the rocks, the mighty Words that would shake the earth, the burning flame in which all worthless things would be destroyed. What was Jesus doing to break the tyranny of Herod Antipas? And so the mighty John was offended at the weakness of Jesus.

John's part was to manœuvre the nation into a corner, to force it to the point where it stood face to face with the Kingdom of God, and so to prepare the people for the coming of Jesus Christ. But why did Jesus not use His power to blast iniquity in high places, to dethrone profane tyranny, to emancipate the people of God? The whole nation was crying out for a mighty redeeming upheaval. Why was Jesus so unconcerned about the great historic destinies of men and nations?

And so John sent messengers to ask Jesus: "Art thou he that should come, or do we look for another?" Jesus answered and said: "Go and show John again the things which ye do hear and see: The blind receive their sight, the lame walk, the lepers are cleansed, the deaf hear, the dead are raised up, and the poor have the Gospel preached unto them."

John had failed to understand the violence of God, the violence of the Gospel of grace. He failed to understand that in Jesus that which was stronger than wind or earthquake or fire had come among men, for in Jesus the still small Voice of God had become flesh and blood.

Let us make no mistake. Jesus did not repudiate the preaching of John the Baptist, that the Kingdom of God would come in power and judgment. Indeed, Jesus took up the preaching of the Baptist and emphasised the fact that the Kingdom will break in with violence. It storms its way into the hearts of men, and only men of violence, men of purpose and determination, enter in—but it is the violence of God, not the violence of men that counts. The Kingdom of

God exerts its power not as men imagine it, not by natural forces such as wind or earthquake or fire, not even by mighty blasts of nuclear energy, but by the still small Voice of the Gospel.

That is the astonishing paradox about Jesus Christ—and the thing that completely baffled John the Baptist: that the violence of the Kingdom of God exerts itself in the suffering patience and humiliation and gentleness of Jesus. Right from the Jordan to Calvary He was led as a lamb to the slaughter.

To see how the gentleness and weakness of Jesus are the violence of the Kingdom of God, go for a moment to Pilate's Judgment Hall. There stands One before Pilate and His accusers who never lifted a violent finger against anyone, and yet on that day the meek and lowly Jesus becomes the centre of a volcanic disturbance that has shaken the world to its foundations. Watch Jesus before His accusers. When He is reviled, He reviles not again. He gives His back to the smiters, His cheek to those that pluck out the hair. As a sheep before her shearers is dumb, so He opens not His mouth. The incredible thing is this: the meeker and milder Jesus is, the more violent the crowd becomes in resentment. The more like a Lamb He is, the more like ravening wolves they become. What is there about this meekness, this prisoner in chains, what is there about the weakness of this Jesus that stirs the passions of men as never before in all history? How is it that by His very suffering and meekness and gentleness Jesus seems to impart passion to men and call forth violence from men, until at last they lay violent hands upon Him and drag Him off to bitter execution?

What happened there?

Jesus was the embodiment on earth of the still small Voice of God, and in Jesus as never before that voice penetrated into the secrets of men and exposed them. The more He stood before them, the more the power of God stormed its way into the citadel of the human soul. Before the weakness and gentleness of Jesus all barriers are broken down, all the thoughts and intents of the heart are revealed. What wind and earthquake and fire could not do, Jesus did: He stormed into the proud heart of man and laid it bare. And He produced the most violent reaction which culminated in the Cross. And so it has been ever since.

Let us not be deceived. The violence of Pilate's Judgment Hall, and the violence of Calvary, were not a mistake. Jesus intended them. He deliberately provoked them, because He came to deal with the sin of man at its worst and to bear it in vicarious passion and atonement. But He provoked them also because it is in their determined and violent reaction that the Kingdom of God lays hold upon men. Mark you, it is a violent reaction provoked by gentleness and love and grace and meekness and suffering, but it is a definite and determined reaction. That is the way in which the Kingdom of God storms its way into the hearts of men.

How does the Kingdom of God come? When the violent take it by force, says Jesus, when men of determined purpose lay violent hands upon it. When the Gospel is preached in the take-it-or-leave-it style, the Kingdom does not come. But when the Gospel is preached in such a way as to force a decision, as to force men to make up their minds about it with determination, or, as the text reads, with violence, then the Kingdom comes.

What was the situation in which Jesus found Himself among His contemporaries? They refused to make up their minds, and evaded decision. That was the last thing they wanted. They were like children in the market-place who would play neither at funerals nor marriages. They would have nothing to do either with the sternness of the Baptist or the homeliness of Jesus. But Jesus continued to body forth in their midst the still small Voice of God, and to exert the pres-

sure of its gentleness and grace upon men until the reaction
came, and it came with violence. Either there was the
volcanic reaction of Calvary with its utter denial and repudi-
ation of Christ and we have been thinking of that, or there
was a reaction of a different sort, another kind of violence.
Some were so offended that they gnashed their teeth and
took up stones to kill Him, but others believed, and said never
man spake like this Man, wondering at the gracious words
that fell from His lips. To some the still small Voice was
thunder, but to others it was the music of angels—but always
there was violence. Men and women were singled out from
the crowd and they too laid violent hands upon Jesus and
would not let Him go until He healed and forgave them.

Think of that day when Jesus went striding through
Jericho on His way to Jerusalem, to Pilate and to Calvary—
and two blind men sat at the road-side crying: "Thou Son of
David, have mercy on us." Jesus walked on unheeding. He
did not even glance over His shoulder at them. It was when
they cried the more earnestly "Thou Son of David, have
mercy on us," that He stopped and healed them.

Or think of that day when the Syro-Phoenician woman
half mad with anguish over her demon-ridden daughter,
shrieked after Him in a way that upset the disciples, but
Jesus made to go on as if He had not heard at all, and heeded
not the cry of pain. It was only when she became violent
that Jesus turned, marvelling at the unparalleled faith He
had provoked: "O woman, great is thy faith: be it unto thee
even as thou wilt."

But think especially of the third day after Calvary when
Jesus as a Stranger joined the company of two disciples on
the way to Emmaus. He talked gently with them, the still
small Voice of God causing their hearts to burn within them.
At Emmaus He made as though He would go further and
only turned aside to abide with them when they constrained

Him—and St. Luke uses the very word for violence in our text and even strengthens it to emphasise the violent hands those disciples laid on Jesus. It was then that the Kingdom broke on their vision in its full glory, and Jesus was made known unto them in the breaking of bread.

The paradox about Jesus is always this: He is never rude or violent in our sense. He never barges in upon a man's soul. He stands without and knocks gently, and even makes as though He would pass by. And yet there is a gentle violence about His meekness that forces us to be violent if we would have Him. We must rise up and react with determination if we would know Him. We must lay violent hands on Him if the Kingdom of God is to come into our lives with power. Is that not the message of these words, "The kingdom of heaven suffers violence, and men of violence take it by force"? You cannot have Jesus in your life except by passionate and determined conviction. You must rise up and choose Him with all your heart and mind and soul and strength.

And yet we must never forget that this is only half the truth. The Kingdom of God suffers our violence because it actively intervenes in our rebellious alienation from God, but it is through that intervention by suffering that it presses in upon us and takes us by storm. Thus behind the fact that the Kingdom comes as it suffers violence at our hands lies the primary fact that the Kingdom is itself the source of all saving action; behind all our reactions lies the primary action of God in His condescending to enter into our human situation in order to act upon us from within. This has two very important things to teach us.

(*a*) Because God condescends to act within our human situation, in His mighty action He adapts Himself to our capacities and accommodates Himself both to our weaknesses and to our violence. With what mighty gentleness God adapts Himself to little children, for they are also of the Kingdom of

God although they are not capable of any violent reactions but can only lie passively in His arms where they are laid by their mothers. Likewise God in Christ adapts Himself to all His little ones, whether they be little children, or the weak, or the frail, or the blind. He does not quench the smoking flax or break the bruised reed, but blesses the poor in spirit and freely bestows upon them the Kingdom of Heaven. But to men of determined purpose the Kingdom adapts itself accordingly, and breaks in upon them in their decisions and actions and calls forth from them a violent reaction. And yet in both cases, to the meek and to the determined, to the frail and to the violent, it is the same Jesus who intervenes, and in both cases He intervenes in the same gentleness and meekness and with the same patience and grace. Therefore, just as His mightiness is gentle with the frail and the meek, so His gentleness is mighty with the violent and the strong.

(*b*) Because in suffering the Kingdom still takes the initiative, because even in all the violence it is the gentleness of grace that remains in absolute control, Jesus reveals himself to those who have laid hold on Him with determined and passionate conviction that they have not chosen Him, but He has chosen them. His grace holds on to us in all the decisions it provokes from us until we acknowledge that we only love Him because He first loved us. The man who is justified by grace is the only one who really knows that he is a lost and helpless sinner, unable to justify himself even by faith, whereas the man who has not received forgiveness thinks that he can justify himself before God or at least co-operate in his own salvation. Similarly, the man who has come to choose Christ with all his heart and mind and soul and strength is the only one who really knows how incapable he is in himself of faith and love towards Jesus Christ, whereas the man who has not received Jesus Christ as his Saviour imagines that he is free to make a decision regarding his own salvation. The

Kingdom of God submits itself to our decisions, and calls them forth, suffering their violence, but at the same time it reveals that what saves us is not what we do, but what God alone does. "Herein is love, not that we loved God but that he loved us, and sent his Son to be the propitiation for our sins." Because it is by suffering love that the Kingdom of God presses in upon us, men of determined purpose and decision enter in only when they become "as little children", relying not at all upon their own strength of will or their own decision of faith but only on the mercy of the Heavenly Father. "Lord, I believe: help thou my unbelief."

CHAPTER III

THE APPROACH TO GOD

"Now Moses was keeping the flock of Jethro his father in law, the priest of Midian; and he led the flock to the back of the wilderness, and came to the mountain of God, unto Horeb. And the angel of the Lord appeared unto him in a flame of fire out of the midst of a bush: and he looked, and, behold, the bush burned with fire, and the bush was not consumed. And Moses said, I will turn aside now, and see this great sight, why the bush is not burned. And when the Lord saw that he turned aside to see, God called unto him out of the midst of the bush, and said, Moses, Moses. And he said, Here am I. And he said, Draw not nigh hither: put off thy shoes from off thy feet, for the place whereon thou standest is holy ground. Moreover he said, I am the God of thy father, the God of Abraham, the God of Isaac, and the God of Jacob. And Moses hid his face; for he was afraid to look upon God. And the Lord said, I have surely seen the affliction of my people which are in Egypt, and have heard their cry by reason of their taskmasters; for I know their sorrows; and I am come down to deliver them out of the hand of the Egyptians, and to bring them up out of that land unto a good land and a large, unto a land flowing with milk and honey; unto the place of the

Canaanite, and the Hittite, and the Amorite, and the Perizzite, and the Hivite, and the Jebusite. And now, behold, the cry of the children of Israel is come unto me: moreover I have seen the oppression wherewith the Egyptians oppress them. Come now therefore, and I will send thee unto Pharoah, that thou mayest bring forth my people the children of Israel out of Egypt. And Moses said unto God, Who am I, that I should go unto Pharaoh, and that I should bring forth the children of Israel out of Egypt? And he said, Certainly I will be with thee; and this shall be the token unto thee, that I have sent thee: when thou hast brought forth the people out of Egypt, ye shall serve God upon this mountain. And Moses said unto God, Behold, when I come unto the children of Israel, and shall say unto them, The God of your fathers hath sent me unto you; and they shall say to me, What is his name? what shall I say unto them? And God said unto Moses, I AM THAT I AM: and he said, Thus shalt thou say unto the children of Israel, I AM hath sent me unto you. And God said moreover unto Moses, Thus shalt thou say unto the children of Israel, The LORD, the God of your fathers, the God of Abraham, the God of Isaac, and the God of Jacob, hath sent me unto you: this is my name for ever, and this is my memorial unto all generations."   Exodus 3, 1-15.

"So Jesus cometh to Simon Peter. He saith unto him, Lord, dost thou wash my feet? Jesus answered and said unto him, What I do thou knowest not now; but thou shalt understand hereafter. Peter saith unto him, Thou shalt never wash my feet. Jesus answered him, If I Wash thee not, thou hast no part with me."
                                                            John 13, 6-8.

During the war I spent a fortnight's holiday exploring the Sinai peninsula in the company of several friends. It was a very wonderful experience, going over the ground where the children of Israel were led thousands of years ago in their pilgrimage to Mt. Sinai. The story of that pilgrimage and above all the account of Moses himself filled my thoughts, and the tremendous sense of the holiness of God which was his. Night after night we made our camp in the wilderness, and as the darkness fell we gathered sticks of acacia and camel-thorn, the dry sapless bushes of the desert, with which to make a fire. They burned up ever so quickly and brilliantly, but almost as soon they died away. They had so little substance that when kindled they were consumed almost immediately.

I always thought of Moses when that happened, and his astonishment at the fire in the desert bush that did not die down. But what was even more astonishing was that the bush itself was not consumed but remained intact and quite undamaged.

What is the meaning of the burning bush that was not consumed? *Nec tamen consumebatur*, the word which the Church of Scotland has taken so closely to itself? Usually that is interpreted to signify the Church in the fires of affliction that is not consumed. That is perhaps a legitimate extension of the meaning and it is certainly as true as it is a beautiful idea. The thorn-bush alight with the flame may well be taken as a symbol of the Church, but the fire is not to be taken as the symbol of affliction, except perhaps when affliction is used by God to bring His own holy presence into the midst of the Church. The symbol of the undying flame and the accompanying voice out of it have one and the same meaning. The burning flame refers to God Himself, the God of whom the New Testament as well as the Old Testament says: "Our God is a consuming fire."

What was it that Moses saw in the burning bush? What are we to see in it? Fire that is steady and undying, fire that burns and does not burn away, fire that has no tendency to destruction in its own nature, and fire that is not consumed by its own activity. Surely all that may well be taken as a symbol of the One divine Being whose being derives its law and its life from itself, the Self-originating, the Self-existing Being, the Living God. Out of the burning bush there came a voice, the voice of the eternal God revealing Himself and giving His own name: "*I am that I am.*" Those words are so pregnant with meaning that it is difficult to give them adequate expression in English. "I am that I am", but also, "I shall be what I shall be", "I am who I am, who was, who is, and who shall be, the ever-living One." Both the voice and the undying flame refer to the One who lives for ever, the flame and the voice matching one another in revealing the eternal *I am*, who lives and loves for ever, whose resources are inexhaustible and whose power is unwearied. He is "the eternal God, the Lord . . . who fainteth not neither is weary." He is the great *I am* to whom all created beings flee for refuge and life and salvation, for they who wait upon Him will renew their strength. And so we hear the same voice in the Old Testament: "I am the first and the last, saith the Lord, and beside me, there is no Saviour"; and in the New Testament: "I am the first and the last, saith the Lord . . . I am He that liveth and was dead, and behold I am alive for ever more." "He that believeth on me, though he were dead, yet shall he live." That is the eternal miracle of all that comes into immediate contact with the living God—even though we are dead yet shall we live.

Think of the ragged, sapless thorn-bush, dried up and half-dead in the sands of the desert; it was not too humble to hold the living God. It was not too gross to burst into flame when He came and not too fragile to be gifted with the treasure of undying Being. The frail little bush burned in the fire of God, and far from being destroyed, it lived anew and lived on as never before. It was nothing at all in itself, and it became the means of the most exalted revelation of God, just like the frail pages of our Bibles today. Out of them also as out of the burning bush there comes the still small Voice of the living God, and our hearts burn within us as it talks to us and reveals the mystery of God's own life and love which He calls us to share in His grace.

But here is a remarkable fact in this Old Testament

I

record that we must consider: The fire of God had no destructive nature—on the contrary it gave life—but immediately Moses approached the burning bush there leapt out of its flames a voice of urgent command: "Draw not nigh hither: put off thy shoes from off thy feet, for the place whereon thou standest is holy ground." Instantly, Moses knew that his life was threatened, and "Moses hid his face; for he was afraid to look upon God"—for no man hath seen God and lived. Now why was it that although the fire carried no threat to the desert bush, but rather enhanced its life, yet when Moses came near, it terrified him, and menaced his soul? Burning in this bush and not consuming it was the eternal flame of the life of God, the power of an endless life, the inexhaustible source of love. This is the very God to whom all men aspire, and for whom our mortal souls pant. Human beings grow weary and decay and crumble away into the dust, but here is the fountain of unending life, life that burns like a fire, so gentle that it does not burn or consume. If that life of God were to take up its dwelling in us, we too should possess the power of endless life, without any threat of decay or of being undone. A man who has such a God for his God has a bond with life that cannot be broken. Such a communion in life with such a God is in its very nature unaffected by the accident of death. It is a sharing in the endless life of God Himself. Who does not thirst for such communion with the living God?

Moses draws near, but immediately he is thrust back, and he is afraid, because he is a sinner. He is unclean, and God is infinitely holy, and in the presence of sin even God's love is as a consuming fire. That is the paradox with which we too are confronted when we hear God's Voice speaking to us out of the holy Scriptures, and then echoing in our conscience. God is the living and the loving God, who seeks and creates fellowship between Himself and us, and yet our conscience is afraid, and will not look upon God. How are we, then, to approach Him? How can we share in the life and the love which He offers to us, who are sinners?

The Word of God speaking to us out of this Old Testament record, has at least two distinct things to tell us about the sinner's approach to God. (1) We cannot approach God in the attitude of spectators. Moses said: "I will turn aside now, and see this great sight, why the bush is not burnt. And when the Lord saw that he turned aside to see, God called unto him out of the midst of the bush, and said: Moses, Moses. And he said: Here am I." (2) We cannot appproach God with unclean feet. And God said: "Draw not nigh hither: put off thy shoes from off thy feet, for the place whereon thou standest is holy ground."

The sinner defends himself in the presence of God by taking up the attitude of a spectator. A spectator is an onlooker. He is not one who really wants to be concerned; he just looks on. He refuses to assume any personal responsibility; he acts as if he does not take part in the matter. When sin makes a man stand off a bit from God, and look on like that in a third personal way, sin is being most subtle and terribly clever: it is evading implication or personal responsibility before God. But when sin does that, it intensifies itself, and fortifies itself. By entrenching itself in the spectator-attitude, it increases its own guilt tenfold. That is the hardest fact about sin—its obdurateness, its brazenness. The unclean heart recoils upon itself and looks out only to look on.

How does God react to the self-defence of sin? The God who dwells in the burning bush is infinitely gentle. His Holy flame does not hurt or consume even the humble thorn bush. His holy love will not hurt the bruised reed, or quench the smoking flax, but when the sinner turns himself into a spectator before God, the gentleness of God burns him, and the love of God consumes him. God is indeed the I AM THAT I AM,

He who is unchanging in the fulness of His divine life and love, with whom we yearn for communion; but when we come with uncleanness in our hearts, or upon our feet, and when that uncleanness makes us standoffish and spectator-like, God's fire hurts us and burns us.

This Old Testament passage, however, has something else to tell us. Moses turned aside to have a look at the spectacle. He was, if you like, like a man who goes to the theatre to look on, not to act, not to take part, but to sit and look in silence. But God will not allow him to do that. Immediately, a voice rings out: "Moses, Moses", and Moses said "Here am I." In other words, God speaks to Moses face to face. He breaks through his defences, and forces him out of his spectator-attitude. Moses must respond, and give to God an answer in direct personal encounter.

That is the way God always deals with us. For long, He may hold Himself back, directing our ways even when we are unaware of it, bringing us to the point for which, in His patience, He has waited, when He may speak to us face to face. God is infinitely gentle with the penitent sinner who hears God calling him by name, and who answers in tears and shame. With such a sinner, there is always the miracle of the burning bush: God's holy flame burns in the midst of his heart, and he is not consumed. But the sinner who does not answer God, who still tries to evade God by looking on, refusing to be implicated, can only be consumed. It is the love of God that consumes him, the God who in love insists on giving Himself to the sinner, whether he will have Him or not; but this love can only resist the defences of the sinner, and judge him. It is not that God wishes to condemn him, and so for long He waits to be gracious; He waits to find the moment when He can pour Himself out in love to the sinner without hurting or consuming him. And if the sinner dares to approach God idly or indifferently or in wilful hypocrisy, or even in unconscious self-defence, God halts him, lest he should dash himself upon the unchanging holiness and love of God.

God cannot hold Himself back for ever, or rather the sinner cannot live for ever entrenched in his independence, surrounded by all the defences which he builds around his mortal life, in order to protect himself from God. So long as he lives on earth, he can hide himself in time, for as long as he is in time, God waits to have mercy upon him. But when he passes out of time into eternity, all his defences fall away from him, and he stands naked before God. But in eternity he has no time for decision, for repentance, or for faith. In time he has time for decision and repentance and faith, for in time the voice of God calls to him and gives him time to make up his mind, and to answer. But when he passes from time into eternity, then all that has gone on in his soul comes to its ultimate crisis. Once that crisis begins, as so many of the parables of Jesus tell us, there is no time for preparation or action. It all happens in a flash, in a moment, in the twinkling of an eye. It is like the swoop of an eagle, the fierce blaze of lightning from one side of the sky to the other, or the bursting of the flood. What time is there to decide or repent, between the flash of the lightning and the crash of thunder, between our exit from time and entry into eternity? Until then, God's voice does not cease to call us, and it is always the pleading of His love, or the command to halt, to take the shoes off our feet, for between us and God the ground is holy. Only the penitent and the forgiven can walk upon it and draw near to the ever-living and ever-loving God who kindles in them the fire of eternal life and does not at all consume them.

Now turn to the passage from the New Testament which we have set beside the account of Moses at the burning bush. It gives us the story of Jesus, at the Last Supper, washing the disciples' feet, one by one, till he comes to Peter. And "Peter saith unto him, Thou shalt never wash my feet. Jesus answered him, If I wash thee not, thou hast no part with me."

Who is this Jesus? He is none other than the God of the burning bush, the Lord of eternal life, the Lord of everlasting love, the "I am that I am". Listen to His voice coming out of the pages of the New Testament: "Before Abraham was, I am. I am the Light of the world. I am the door. I am the Good Shepherd. I am the bread of life. I am the way, the truth, and the life. I AM."

It is the same living God, come down, condescending to our lowly estate in infinite gentleness and yet in infinite majesty. The same fire flames within Him as flamed within the burning bush, and the frail earthly body is not consumed by the fire. The time for the manifestation of the divine Majesty in a desert bush or on Mt. Sinai is past. Now God condescends to dwell permanently in a human life, not simply to use the human life as the instrument of His manifestation but to take it up into Himself and identify Himself with it for ever, Jesus Christ, very God, and very Man in one Person. He the Son of Man is now "the burning bush", or rather instead of the burning bush: in Him there flames forth the same gentle fire of Almighty Holy Love, and out of Him there comes forth the same voice of the eternal I AM.

Now the fire of God moves among men, mingling freely with sinners. See how gentle He is with the fallen, the crushed, the wounded, the outcast, how patient with the weak, how tender with the penitent. But see Him, see the same fire, moving among the self-righteous, the hardened and the proud, and listen to His voice—did ever words burn with such a flame as His? And yet He is not come to condemn, but to save. The fire that flames undying with Him has no tendency to destroy in its own nature. He is Light whose nature it is to enlighten, and if He consumes the darkness it is only by sending forth His light into its midst. He is Life whose nature it is to quicken and if He destroys the old it is only in sending forth His life to impart the new. He is Love whose nature it is to pour itself out in grace upon all, and if He resists any in wrath, it is only the resistance of love to everything that is against love.

And so Jesus stands forth as the manifestation, as the actual embodiment among men, of the divine Light, Life, and Love, He in whom the fulness of the Godhead dwells bodily, the I Am That I Am on earth. He stands forth and claims to be able to satisfy all the aspirations of men, all the hunger and thirst of their soul for the living and loving God: "Come unto me all ye that labour and are heavy laden, and I will give you rest." He is the living God who has not waited for sinners to approach Him, but who has approached them and teaches them how to approach God by finding in Himself the way to the Father. Above all He gathers from among sinners twelve about Him, and teaches them the Way, the Truth and the Life, that they may teach others how the sinner may draw near to the living God, and live.

That is what we see so clearly here in the midst of the Supper on the night before the Lord is crucified. Think of it in relation to the lessons we learned from the Old Testament passage: "Draw not nigh hither: put off thy shoes from off thy feet, for the place whereon thou standest is holy ground." We cannot come before God unclean, and we cannot come before God as spectators. Now listen to the message from this New Testament passage, in which Jesus washes the feet of the disciples and makes them clean, and in which through the Holy Supper He gives them to participate in the life and love of God.

The washing recalled to the disciples their baptism, once and for all with its promise of complete cleansing that did not need repeating, but now this solemn act of washing the feet is meant to prepare the disciples to accompany Christ and watch with Him as He treads alone the holy ground between sinful man and Holy God that He may make atonement and open up a new and living way in Himself for all men freely and boldly to draw near to the Father. By this feet-washing at the hands of Jesus in utter humiliation, they are taught that sinful man draws near to God only through the amazing grace and humiliation of God. This takes place in the midst of the Supper, before the holy of holies in it, in which Jesus shares His own cup with the disciples, and breaks His own bread with them, in intercession with the Father that they may all be consecrated together in one, by that which He is about to undertake on their behalf. And so Jesus binds the disciples closely to Himself with solemn and sacramental bonds, that as He goes forth to His lonely Cross, the disciples may not look on as mere spectators. When at last they stand before the Cross, they will stand as men who have already been made to eat His broken body and drink His shed blood, and will watch as those who have part and lot in it all, for He dies for them, as their Mediator, as their High Priest, as their Saviour. Although now He is alone on the Cross, and they, the disciples, stand among the sinners who crucified Him, and though the awful chasm of their sin divides them from Him their beloved Lord, they know that it is this very sin and shame of theirs which binds them to Him and Him to them for ever, because it is this very sin and shame that He has taken upon Himself, that they with Him may together draw near to the Holy and loving Father.

The message of the Old Testament is reiterated and reinforced by the New: we cannot come before God unclean; we cannot come before God as spectators but only in direct personal encounter. But here in the New Testament message we find that the same God has come to us in Jesus to bring about that personal encounter, to wash us and make us clean, which we cannot do of ourselves, and even to give us to participate in the very life of God by holy communion in the Man of Calvary.

CHAPTER IV

THE CLEANSING OF THE FELLOWSHIP

"Now before the feast of the passover, Jesus knowing that his hour was come that he should depart out of this world unto the Father, having loved His own which were in the world, he loved them unto the end. And during supper, the devil having already put into the heart of Judas Iscariot, Simon's son, to betray him, Jesus, knowing that the Father had given all things into his hands, and that he came forth from God, and goeth unto God, riseth from supper, and layeth aside his garments; and he took a towel and girded himself. Then he poureth water into the bason, and began to wash the disciples' feet, and to wipe them with the towel wherewith he was girded. So he cometh to Simon Peter. He saith unto him, Lord, dost thou wash my feet? Jesus answered, and said unto him, What I do thou knowest not now; but thou shalt understand hereafter. Peter saith unto him, Thou shalt never wash my feet. Jesus answered him, If I wash thee not, thou hast no part with me. Simon Peter saith unto him, Lord, not my feet only, but also my hands and my head. Jesus saith to him, He that is bathed needeth not save to wash his feet, but is clean every whit: and ye are clean, but not all. For he knew him that should betray him; therefore said he, Ye are not all clean. So when He had washed their feet, and taken his garments, and sat down again, he said unto them, Know ye what I have done to you? Ye call me, Master, and, Lord: and ye say well; for so I am. If I then, the Lord and the Master, have washed your feet, ye also ought to wash one another's feet. For I have given you an example, that ye also should do as I have done to you. Verily, verily, I say unto you, A servant is not greater than his lord; neither one that is sent greater than he that sent him. If ye know these things, blessed are ye if ye do them."   John 13, 1-17.

Sometimes St. John appears to have written his Gospel with the deliberate intention of filling out the material given in the others, and usually gives an account that is more doctrinal and more from the inner understanding of the various incidents. Sometimes too he presupposes that his readers know what has taken place and does not therefore need to describe all the details. For example, in his account of the Baptism of Jesus he does not actually mention the detail of Jesus' baptism in water, but it is quite definitely assumed. So here at the Last Supper John presupposes our knowledge of the actual institution of the Supper, and is concerned to fill out the account of it that we may have a deeper understanding of it all, adding in particular this incident of the feet-washing, as well as the discourses Jesus gave at the Table, and the "high-priestly" prayer of Christ, which is the other and inner side of the Lord's Supper, recorded in the seventeenth chapter. In order to get a full understanding of this passage, therefore, we have to reconstruct the whole story with the aid of the other Gospels.

Jesus and His disciples were in the upper room having a meal, either the passover meal or one in anticipation of it. It was in the midst of this meal that He instituted the sacrament of the Last Supper. During the earlier part of the meal a dispute arose among the disciples about precedence, and it was at this point that Jesus intervened and said: "Who is greater, he that sits at meat, or he that serves? But I am among you as he that serves." Then before the most sacred part of the meal, Jesus arose, and while the others were reclining at the Table, He proceeded to wash the disciples' feet. It was a most solemn moment, and particularly significant because it took place not at the very beginning but apparently just before the institution of the Sacrament of His body and blood.

We have already considered two of the lessons that Jesus wanted to teach His disciples about the sinner's approach to

God on the holy ground of atonement, that he must be made clean through Christ, and that he must draw near not as a spectator but as a participator. But there are several more lessons we are to learn from this passage about drawing near to God in Christ.

(1) There is no room for pride in the worship of God. How could there be when we draw near to God in His abasement and humiliation in Jesus Christ?

It was not very often that Jesus was dramatic. This was one of the few occasions. He felt that something specially solemn was needed to bring home to the disciples the lesson of humility and to show the kind of God they had to do with. What could have been more effective than for the disciples to see their Lord and God on His knees washing their dirty feet? What a revelation of divine Majesty in abject humiliation, engaged in an act of menial service, in order to cleanse His sinful creatures! How could anyone be proud who has seen Jesus on His knees?

Peter was aghast—and, it would appear, for a two-fold reason. He was aghast at the self-abasement of Jesus, the Lord and Master whom he worshipped and adored. It was unthinkable that Christ the Son of the living God should condescend to wash his dirty feet, and Peter knew himself to be unclean. But Peter was aghast for another reason: he himself was humiliated beyond words. What could be more humiliating than to have Jesus do him such a menial service? (The husband who feels humiliated when his wife brushes his shoes, may perhaps feel a tiny fraction of Peter's humiliation.) Peter was not a proud man. He was a frank, open-hearted person, ready to acknowledge his weakness and sin, but for all that, there was a deep element of pride lodged within him, and the action of Jesus touched it, and made it hurt. That was part of his washing. Before Calvary came, before the Lord's Supper came, Jesus wanted to teach Peter and all the disciples that pride is the deadliest and the deepest of all sins; and He wanted to cleanse them from pride, that with meekness and purity and poverty of spirit they might look upon the Lord on the Cross and in the midst of their horror and shame understand its meaning.

It is important to see that what made Peter aghast at Jesus was not any vice in his heart, but his very virtue. "Lord, dost thou wash my feet?" But it was virtue gone wrong. When virtue resents the humiliation of Jesus, when virtue resents the Cross of Christ as it had done at least on one notable occasion before in Peter's life, then virtue becomes the stronghold of sin. That is a hard lesson to learn, because it is in the sphere of virtue that we have our toughest struggle with Jesus. It is there that we are so often unbowed in our pride, and that we need to be washed and made clean most of all. When we see Jesus on His knees girded like a servant to wash our feet, we learn that even our goodness is unclean in His sight. When we go to Holy Communion and share in His body and blood, we feel shame for our whole being, for our good as well as for our evil. He who does not admit that, who can actually protest at the Table of the Lord, that only part of him needs cleansing, that Jesus did not die for all of him but only for some of him, is still unbowed before the Cross, still a fundamentally unforgiven and unsaved man. The abasement of Jesus at the Supper and on the Cross teaches us that though He was rich, He became poor for our sakes that we through His poverty might be made rich—through His poverty and humiliation. When He exchanges His riches for our poverty, He measures our poverty by the incredible extent of His impoverishment and abasement: He was made a curse for us that we might be made the righteousness of God in Him. When we receive His riches extended to us in the Holy Supper we can receive them only with the acknowledgment that we are utterly destitute and poor and naked, and covered only with shame. Only so are we clothed with His grace.

(2) There is a two-fold washing needed for our approach to God.

When Peter realised his mistake, and realised that he could have no part or lot with Jesus, he asked to have not only his feet but his hands and his head washed as well. Jesus answered: "He that is bathed needeth not save to wash his feet." Perhaps that may mean: "This is a symbolic act, Peter, and the washing of the feet stands for the washing of the whole body. It is quite sufficient for your feet to be washed." So in Baptism we use water symbolically, and it is sufficient to use but a little to signify the cleansing of the person baptised, or his death and resurrection with Christ, just as at a burial we cast only three handfuls of earth symbolically upon the grave during the act of committal. It is the symbolic act that is religiously and sacramentally significant.

But the real meaning, I think, lies deeper. When a person is baptised, that is the sign and seal of the fact that in Jesus Christ he is made clean every whit, that once for all Christ's promise of forgiveness and justification is extended, and that promise given in the Name of Father, Son and Holy Spirit is never withdrawn. As the sign and seal of that promise Baptism does not need to be repeated; indeed to repeat it is to call in question the divine promise and to dishonour the divine Name in which Baptism is solemnly given. Baptism does not need to be repeated any more than Calvary needs to be repeated, and indeed to repeat Baptism is to put Christ to an open shame and crucify to ourselves the Son of God afresh, as the writer of the Epistle to the Hebrews puts it. Nothing can undo the Cross, and nothing can undo the fact of Baptism. But we know that every time we come into the House of God, or come to Holy Communion, we need cleansing again and again. That does not mean that we need reconverting or rebaptising, but it means that we have to appropriate continually what has been extended to us once and for all. It means that we need fresh humiliation, fresh forgiveness and continued sanctification.

It was at this Supper, when they had broken bread and shared the cup together that Christ engaged in His intercessory prayer which we are allowed to overhear in the seventeenth chapter. And there we hear Christ say that He has sanctified Himself for our sakes, that we might be sanctified in Him. Our forgiveness and sanctification cannot be separated or detached from Christ Himself. He is Himself our forgiveness and sanctification, and therefore though He has once and for all died for us to forgive and sanctify us in Himself, we are given continually to partake of it through communion with Him. And so here at the Last Supper, just before it begins, Jesus deliberately washes the disciples' feet to indicate that here in Holy Communion with Him, the cleansing which He has once and for all promised us, and once and for all fulfilled on the Cross, He renews to us. As often as we go to the Holy Table we feed upon His forgiveness and are confirmed in His sanctification.

The washing of the feet is, therefore, to be understood in a sacramental context, and as sharing the sacramental significance of the Last Supper. But as a sacrament always signifies and seals the Word of the Gospel, so the feet-washing is to be understood in terms of the Word of Christ which cleanses and sanctifies us. "What I do, thou knowest not now; but thou shalt understand hereafter," Jesus said to Peter. Though it was perhaps only long after, through the enlightenment of the Holy Spirit, that Peter really came to understand, it was when the cleansing of the feet and the Supper was over that Jesus spoke the Word that gives sacramental depth and meaning to the act. "Now ye are clean through the word that I have spoken unto you." And again in His prayer, "Sanctify them through thy truth. Thy word is truth."

It is as we listen to the Words of Jesus, study their truth, meditate upon them, that we are cleansed and sanctified day by day. That is the way in which our washing in the Blood of Christ, which took place once for all on the Cross, is daily applied to our heart and life. Apart from that Word the cleansing of our feet by water or even the eating of the bread and drinking of the wine in the Lord's Supper means nothing at all. Is that not why John who writes this Gospel of the Word made flesh is so concerned to balance the accounts of the Supper given in the other Gospels by adding here the teaching of Jesus at the Supper, that along with it we may receive His Word, for as Jesus said, it is as we receive His Word that He and the Father come and take up their abode with us and we have communion with them through the Holy Spirit? The lesson we have to learn here is that cleansing and sanctification are given in and through the Word of Christ. They are enclosed in the Word and it is as we receive the Word, as water is applied to our bodies, or as bread and wine are extended to our mouths, that we are given cleansing and sanctification. Cleansing and sanctification are not things that we can possess in ourselves or possess simply by a legal title; they are in Christ who gives Himself to us in His Word. It is through listening to His Word, therefore, through taking heed to it, that we are actually and actively cleansed and sanctified. Quite practically and literally that means that we cannot do without our daily reading of the Bible and our daily meditation upon its truth. It is when we hide the Word of God in our heart that we are kept clean. "Thy word have I hid in my heart that I might not sin against thee", said the Psalmist. There is no other doctrine of daily sanctification in the New Testament than that, except that now it is the Word of God in Christ Jesus, the Word of the Cross which is the power of God.

(3) Jesus bids us wash one another's feet! "If I then, your Lord and Master, have washed your feet, ye also ought to wash one another's feet."

That is something quite unexpected. We cannot even cleanse our own hearts. How can we be expected to cleanse each other? Who can forgive sins but God only? Only Jesus can forgive and wash us, and make us quite clean. That is quite true. But as we have seen, there is a two-fold washing. Jesus Christ died once and for all that through His blood we may be cleansed from all sin. No one can add anything to that. But day by day we need to remind each other of the Gospel, of the Word of Jesus.

We can do that in no other way than in the way in which Jesus Himself did it when He washed the feet of the disciples, for He deliberately did that in order to give them an example in the humble service of the Gospel. Each of us in Christ is made a servant of every other in Christ, and everyone needs the service of others. That applies just as much to the soul as it does to the body, for in spiritual as well as in physical necessities we cannot do without one another. Therefore in the fellowship of the Church of Christ, the ministry of the Gospel to one another should be accompanied by service to one another in material things; and service to one another in material things should have its evangelical counterpart in the ministry of spiritual things. It is in both these ways together that we are to hold up Jesus Christ before one another, and when we do that "we wash one another's feet".

Daily Christian life and fellowship should thus have, as it were, a sacramental character, or at least a two-fold aspect in Christ. On the one hand, we are bidden perform acts of service to one another, even acts of menial, humiliating service. These are the very acts which Jesus uses in cleansing us. Are we not sometimes touched to the heart, indeed shamed and cleansed in heart, when a friend or even a stranger performs a very humble service to us, and so holds up Christ before our very eyes? Such acts are not frequent enough, even among those who love one another dearly, and certainly not frequent enough among the members of our congregations. It is in the fellowship of such humble service that Christ Himself comes into the midst to humble and cleanse us.

On the other hand, we have to speak to one another about Jesus, for we need others to tell us the Word which we cannot really tell ourselves. We cannot very well, for example, tell to ourselves that we are forgiven and cleansed, for we are not able ultimately to disentangle the Word of God from our own desires and wishes, and even when we read the Bible privately we are accustomed to tell ourselves what we think the Bible says rather than to listen to what it says against our own preconceptions and assumptions. We really only hear the Word of God in the Bible when we let it speak against us. But since that is very difficult for us to do, God in His mercy has planted us in the fellowship of the Church, where we have others to tell us His Word and where we too are to tell His Word to others. It is in this mutual telling of the Word of the Gospel that Christ Himself comes and makes us clean through the Word which He speaks and sanctifies us through His truth. In the last book of the Old Testament we read: "Then they that feared the Lord spoke often one to another, and the Lord hearkened, and heard it. And a book of remembrance was written, before him, for them that feared the Lord, and that thought upon his name." That is how we cleanse one another's thoughts, or rather that is how Jesus Christ cleanses our thoughts as we speak to one another about Him.

"If ye know these things, happy are ye if ye do them."

K

IV

THE FAITHFULNESS
OF GOD

CHAPTER I

OUR SURE AND STEADFAST HOPE

"God, being minded to shew more abundantly unto the heirs of the promise the immutability of his counsel, interposed with an oath: that by two immutable things, in which it is impossible for God to lie, we may have a strong encouragement, who have fled for refuge to lay hold of the hope set before us; which we have as an anchor of the soul, a hope both sure and stedfast and entering into that which is within the veil; whither as a forerunner Jesus entered for us, having become a high priest for ever after the order of Melchizedek." Hebrews 6, 17-20.

In this passage the apostolic author tells us that the Christtian hope is as sure and steadfast as the eternal God Himself, for God has pledged Himself to fulfil it. Hope could not have any surer ground than this where God's own Being and Honour are at stake. In order to set this clearly before us the author makes use of two familiar Old Testament traditions.

First, he recalls the fact that when God made His covenant with Abraham, He confirmed His promises of blessing by a solemn oath in order to give him full assurance in hope. When men want to confirm their own declarations to one another in such a way as to remove all hesitation and doubt they seal them with a solemn oath in the name of God as their surety. That is what God has condescended to do with us. Not only has He given us the promise of His blessing and salvation, but He has confirmed it by a solemn oath, and because God can swear by none greater than Himself, He has interposed His own self as surety. In other words, God mediates His promise of salvation to us in such a way that He has pledged His very being, or staked His own existence as immutable God, in its fulfilment. God can no more fail to fulfil His promise than He can cease to be God! That is the strong consolation to which we may flee for refuge to lay hold upon the hope set before us.

Secondly, the author of this epistle recalls the ancient liturgy of the Day of Atonement in which God's covenant-mercies with Israel were renewed year by year. Once a year, at God's command, the high priest, bearing the blood of sacrifice, entered within the veil of the holy of holies to intercede with God for His people and to receive His peace and blessing in the renewal of His covenant-mercies toward them. All Israel's hope from year to year was pinned upon that renewal of the Covenant, but the very fact that it had to be repeated annually showed how imperfect and temporary that rite was. But now in Jesus Christ the Son of God Himself has come to be our High Priest, who not only shed His blood once for all to establish a New Covenant of peace between God and man that does not need to be repeated, but rose again and has entered within the veil into the holy presence of God the Father, anchoring the Covenant in eternity, where it is beyond all imperfection and change, eternal and immutable as God Himself.

In both these ways the writer of this Epistle is saying the same thing: in Jesus Christ God Himself has come into our human life and forged a link between God and man which can never be broken. In the death of Jesus Christ God has pledged Himself as our Saviour, and He can no more go back upon that than He can go back upon the death of His dear Son; but in the resurrection of Jesus Christ, wearing our humanity, our union and communion with God has been secured in the eternal life of God. Jesus Christ Himself, the fact of Christ in His death and now in His endless life, is the immutable ground of our faith and the eternal surety of our salvation. He is our sure and steadfast hope. That is the particular aspect of this passage that we are to consider here.

In Jesus Christ we have a hope set before us, as an anchor
of the soul that enters within the veil. Not only is Jesus Christ
the Priest of the Cross, but He is the Priest of the Resurrection.
Jesus Christ is risen and is yonder, on the other side of the
Cross, on the other side of death, and judgment, and hell,
yonder at the right hand of God; and we are here anchored
to Him, anchored to Him by His incarnation, by His death
and resurrection, and therefore we too are anchored to
yonder within the veil.

What is the veil? It is the veil between the visible and the
invisible, between the temporal and the eternal, between the
present and the future. We are anchored in Jesus to what is on
the other side, and what holds us is sure and steadfast, Jesus
the anchor that will not drag when all the storms of life and
death break over our heads and threaten to destroy us.

That is our unshakable hope. Here, then, is the Church in
this world, embroiled in history on earth with all its trouble
and storms in the wrath of the nations. Yonder is Jesus, risen
from the dead, risen in body, ascended wearing our humanity,
on the other side of corruption and decay, on the other side
of judgment and Calvary, beyond all the powers of darkness
and evil, victorious over them all. And we in the Church of
Christ are securely anchored to Him and to the new life
within the veil. The sheer joy and certainty of that hope are
desperately needed in the world today. Our world is rent with
anxiety and despair. We see it everywhere in the work of the
novelists, the artists, the poets, the musicians, the philosophers
—the gnawing anxiety that will not be stilled, the nameless
threat to our deepest existence, the sense of being suspended
between being and non-being. And so we have our prophets
of doom and disaster whose words bite into our complacency,
speaking of utter annihilation to our world and to our
civilisation by the hydrogen bomb. But the Christian Church
has a hope that is not embarrassed, a hope of irrepressible

certainty and joy imparted to it by Jesus Christ. Even on the way to the Cross He cried out: "Be of good cheer. I have overcome the world!" And now risen from the dead, He inspires His Church with the same confidence and laughing defiance of all darkness and doom.

I know we love to sing so much:

> Lead kindly light, amid the encircling gloom,
>   Lead thou me on,
> The night is dark and I am far from home:
>   Lead thou me on.
> Keep thou my feet: I do not ask to see
> The distant scene,—one step enough for me.

But what has that dismal dirge to do with the resurrection of Jesus Christ and the breathless hope of the New Testament? What has that dim and narrow vision in common with the eager expectation of the advent of Christ and the breaking in of the glory of the ascended Lord to rule over the world of men? Nothing at all. We have to learn again the meaning of the Christian hope, the light that lightens the nations and the glory of God's people, the Church: Jesus Christ the hope of the world!

If we are to regain that hope we must return to Easter, and see the nature and the work of this Jesus. Recall St. John's account of the coming of the risen Jesus to His disciples in the upper room. The first thing Jesus does is to show the disciples His hands and His feet, and the print of the nails in them, and then the sword-wound in His side. They are the marks of His identity. He is the very one whom they had followed so long and known so intimately, the one who three days before had eaten supper with them in that very room, the Jesus who was crucified on the Cross and buried in the tomb, but now that same Jesus risen in body— there are the nail-prints in His flesh. He is risen from the dead in the fulness of His humanity, the Lamb as it had been slain.

That is the basic reason for our hope—the Cross. Jesus Christ the Son of God made flesh for us and our salvation, was crucified to bear and bear away the sin of the world, to break down the barrier between God and man, and to reconcile the world to God. Jesus Christ descended into hell, an awful hell of our sin and guilt and its righteous judgment. He has borne our iniquities and suffered for us in holy sacrifice, that we might be forgiven and restored to the Father as His dear children. That is the deepest reason for our hope, that God has overcome our alienation and reconciled us to Himself.

If our hope is based on reconciliation, it is also true that reconciliation determines the fulfilment of our hope. How can we expect to be heirs of this hope without also entering into all that the Gospel of reconciliation brings and demands? That is a question that belongs to the very heart of evangelism and the ecumenical movement. How can we possibly lay claim to this hope without engaging in the work of the evangel to proclaim it to others? And how can we proclaim that God was in Christ reconciling the world unto Himself without seeking reconciliation with one another? How can we proclaim atonement through the blood of Christ without being at-one among ourselves as Churches? It is impossible. We cannot sincerely preach reconciliation and peace through the Cross and then act a lie against it by refusing to be one Church, and one Body of Christ. To live in disunity is to give the lie to the Gospel of reconciliation. It is a slander upon the blood of Christ. Evangelism and the unity of the Church belong together in the hope that is set before us, for God has already joined them together in the reconciliation of Christ Jesus. What God has joined together, let not man put asunder.

Along with the fact of reconciliation there is another basic reason for our hope—the fact that Jesus Christ crucified for our reconciliation has not only risen from the dead but has ascended in the fulness of His humanity. Yonder at the right hand of God Almighty, yonder in the heart of God, is Jesus who is man as well as Lord and God. He, the Son of God, came into the world to become man, and was made bone of our bone and flesh of our flesh; but when He rose again from the dead, it was as man, as flesh and bone, as real man that He rose. We cannot emphasise enough today the supreme fact of the humanity of the risen Jesus. We do not believe in a Ghost, but in the whole Jesus Christ, fully man, fully God, in Jesus who is risen in body, in real manhood. That is the Jesus who is the substance of our hope and the anchor of our souls. What kind of anchor would we have if we were only tethered to a ghost? If Jesus is only a ghost, and is not now bone of our bone and flesh of our flesh, then the Gospel of Jesus has no weight or substance for us, no relevance at all to us men of flesh and bone on this earth. No, we do not worship some inhuman ghost, we worship and adore Jesus—and that is of the very essence of our hope: that Jesus Christ wearing our humanity, Jesus bone of our bone and flesh of our flesh, is at the right hand of God, and is exalted as Lord and King of all. Because it is our humanity that Jesus wears, you and I are anchored to Him within the veil.

There is a Man on the throne of the universe. He is our man, wearing our humanity. Our name is written in His nail-prints and in His heart. We are anchored to Him, and nothing can break that bond or separate us from Him. There is nothing that can drag Jesus off the throne of God Almighty, nothing that can undo the bond that binds our humanity in Him to Eternity. In Him the love of eternal God has forged a union between God and man, a union in Deity and in perfect Humanity, a union for ever sealed by the blood of the Cross through which all sin and evil and guilt and death have for ever been put away, so that in Him we have a hope that is absolutely sure and steadfast. "We are more than conquerors through him that loved us. For I am persuaded that neither death, nor life, nor angels, nor principalities, nor powers, nor things present, nor things to come, nor height nor depth, nor any other creature, shall be able to separate us from the love of God, which is in Christ Jesus our Lord."

Now let us be more specific, for God has taken care to be more specific with us. Just as He condescended to Abraham to make His great Covenant of grace, not only with solemn promises of blessing and salvation, but solemnly to confirm them with an oath, so in the founding of the New Covenant God has condescended in Christ to give us His solemn pledge in two immutable sacraments in which it is impossible for Him to lie: in *Baptism*, in which Jesus was numbered with us the transgressors to bear our sin, that we being numbered with Him also in baptism may share in His sacrifice; and in the *Lord's Supper* in which Jesus through bread and wine bound us in such communion with Him as He went to the Cross on our behalf, that as often as we eat the bread and drink the wine, we share in the power of His endless life. Not only has God kept His covenant-promise, but He has entirely fulfilled it in Himself when in Jesus Christ He interposed Himself between our sins and Himself, and stood in as our surety to reunite us with Himself. It is that finished work, that fulfilled promise that He freely offers to us in the sacramental ordinances, that through them our hope in Christ may be as an anchor of the soul sure and steadfast and which enters into that within the veil. These ordinances are given to us, therefore, that in and through them we may flee from our own weakness and frailty and take refuge in the immutable faithfulness of God in Jesus.

These sacraments are sacraments not of our faithfulness but of God's faithfulness in Christ Jesus. They require faith from us, and require faithfulness in receiving and using them. We must believe in Jesus Christ as our Lord and Saviour, for we have no inheritance and no hope at all apart from faith in Him. But in His very gift of the Sacraments God tells us that it is not our faithfulness that counts so much as the faithfulness of Christ, not our obedience so much as His obedience on our behalf. It is the part of our faith to rely wholly upon His faithfulness and His obedience. The sacraments are given to us, therefore, as the means whereby we may flee from ourselves and all our unfaithfulness, and take refuge in what He has done and continues to do for us. It is His eternal faithfulness that grasps our faith and holds it, even when we waver and lose hope, for He will never let us go. Here, then, in Baptism and Holy Communion are two immutable things which signify and extend to us the immutable promise of God and His immutable confirmation of it in Himself in the Incarnation and death and resurrection of Jesus Christ, and so they insert into the midst of our feeble and wavering faith the steadfast faithfulness of God who keeps His promises. How can God go back upon the incarnation? How can He turn His back upon the blood of His beloved Son? On the contrary: If God be for us, if God has by these two immutable things sworn to us, binding us in sacramental union with Jesus Christ who died and rose again to be our Saviour, then who can be against us? Who shall lay anything to the charge of God's elect? It is God who justifies us. Who will now rake up our sins and bring us into condemnation? It is Christ who died for us, or rather is risen again, who is even now at the right hand of God, and who also makes intercession for us.

Yes, that also belongs to the sacraments—the advocacy of Jesus Christ, His priestly intercession within the veil. Think again of what St. John had to say about the Last Supper. The other evangelists speak about the actual meal Jesus had with His disciples; but John speaks of the other side of the Last Supper, of Jesus' intercessory prayer. He prayed that we in His Church might be kept, and that we might be one with

Him as He the Incarnate Son and the Father were One, and indeed that through His self-consecration on the Cross we might be consecrated together into one with Him. In one of the other Gospels we get a direct glimpse of what that may mean, in Jesus' words to Peter: "I have prayed for you, that your faith fail not." So Jesus prays for us. His heavenly intercession bears us up before the face of God, and His prayer is heard. So He prayed at the inauguration of the Supper, and so He continues to pray every time we celebrate the Holy Communion in His name, that His Church on earth may be kept, and may be perfected in one as He the Incarnate Son and the Father are One. The sacraments are bonds that enter like that within the veil, and anchor us both to God in Christ, and also bind us into unity with one another in Christ.

That is what happens on the other side, within the veil. What happens on this side of the veil, when we eat the bread and drink the wine? This is what the sacrament declares, and what it declares under the veil of bread and wine is immutably fulfilled within the veil: as surely as we eat this bread and it becomes part of us, and as surely as we drink this wine and it enters into us and becomes part of our flesh and blood, so surely are we through the sacraments anchored and united to Jesus Christ, becoming bone of His bone and flesh of His flesh, everlastingly secured to Him within the veil. He holds on to us and nothing can tear us out of His grasp.

That sure and steadfast hope applies not only to the individual believer but to the Church, which is Christ's Body. The Church is united to Christ, made His very own, His very Body. He will never divorce His Church, even though she proves unfaithful. His love will hold on to her until she is brought at last to be presented to Him as a chaste virgin. And so the Church's hope lies not in itself but in Jesus Christ, who remains faithful and whose everlasting faithfulness is the guarantee and the surety of the Church's hope in Him.

What are we to do about this hope from day to day? What is there to which we can put our hand, and to which we can turn our heart and mind, in our own lives, in our congregations and Churches? Here are three things we can and indeed ought to do.

(1) *We must be ready to give a reason for the hope that is in us*

Let us turn our mind and heart to the Cross of Christ and let it tell us all that God has done for us and for mankind. It is the Cross that tells us finally what Christ has done and what He has perfectly accomplished on our behalf in complete triumph over the powers of darkness and sin and death and hell and wrath and destruction. Let us learn the meaning of the atonement, learn to carry the Word of the Cross about in our heart and be ready at all times to utter it in the ears of our fellows. We must be ready to point others to the Crucified Lord that others too may find in Him their Saviour and share with us in the inheritance of hope in Him.

(2) *We must be obedient to the blood of Christ*

If it is through the blood of Christ that we have peace with God, and through the blood of Christ that we are reconciled to God, then we must resolve to be obedient to it: resolve to live out the atonement by being actually at-one; resolve to seek reconciliation with all for whom Christ died that they might be one in Him. Every time we go to the Table of the Lord and partake of the bread and of the wine, of the body and blood of Christ, let us resolve to go away obedient to the one body broken for us and the one blood shed for us. How can we really and sincerely partake of that holy Sacrament and refuse to sit down together as Churches at the Lord's Table? Surely it is blasphemy for Churches to partake of that one body and one blood and yet to refuse to unite with one another. By this broken body and this shed blood God has given Himself utterly to heal and reconcile us, and make us one in Him; by the very same body and the very same blood we are bound to seek unity, and from day to day to live out at-one-ment or reconciliation between all who are divided from God and from each other, Church and Church, employers and employees, class and class (how dreadful that we should have to use such terms), nation and nation. Blessed are the peace-makers, for theirs is the Kingdom of Heaven, blessed indeed, for it is through the blood of Christ that we have such peace.

(3) *We must bear a joyful witness to the risen and advent Lord*

This same Jesus will come again, and come wearing our humanity. He will come to judge and renew the world. We cannot tell all that He will do when He comes in judgment and renewal, but He will undoubtedly judge our divisions, and expose the lies which we have acted out against the unity of His body and blood and uncover the hypocrisy of all who in the name of truth perpetuated division and slew peace among their brethren. He will come also to heal and renew His Church, to bind up its wounds as well as to cut away its corruption. To the Church that hopes in the risen Lord against hope, that believes in His faithfulness against all its own unfaithfulness, to the Church that flies from its own inadequacy and failure to lay hold upon the hope of His resurrection, He will certainly come to renew the heaven and the earth and bring to a glorious consummation the whole purpose of His love and creation. Surely it is time we learned to share again with the Church of the New Testament its irrepressible gladness in the risen Lord and its eager expectation of His coming again, when He who rose again in body, will come not only to refresh our souls but to renew the whole creation visible and invisible as the theatre of His glory.

CHAPTER II

THE PATIENCE OF JESUS

". . . And these all, having had witness borne to them through their faith, received not the promise, God having provided some better thing concerning us, that apart from us they should not be made perfect.

"Therefore let us also, seeing we are compassed about with so great a cloud of witnesses, lay aside every weight, and the sin which doth so easily beset us, and let us run with patience the race that is set before us, looking unto Jesus the author and perfecter of our faith, who for the joy that was set before him endured the cross, despising shame, and hath sat down at the right hand of the throne of God, For consider him that hath endured such gainsaying of sinners against themselves, that ye wax not weary, fainting in your souls, Ye have not yet resisted unto blood, striving against sin: and ye have forgotten the exhortation which reasoneth with you as with sons. My son, regard not lightly the chastening of the Lord, nor faint when thou art reproved of him; for whom the Lord loveth he chasteneth, and scourgeth every son whom he receiveth. It is for chastening that ye endure; God dealeth with you as with sons; for what son is there whom his father chasteneth not? But if ye are without chastening, whereof all have been made partakers, then are ye bastards, and not sons. Furthermore, we had the fathers of our flesh to chasten us, and we gave them reverence: shall we not much rather be in subjection unto the Father of spirits, and live? For they verily for a few days chastened us as seemed good to them; but he for our profit, that we may be partakers of his holiness. All chastening seemeth for the present to be not joyous, but grievous: yet afterward it yieldeth peaceable fruit unto them that have been exercised thereby, even the fruit of righteousness. Wherefore lift up the hands that hang down, and the palsied knees; and make straight the paths for your feet, that that which is lame be not turned out of the way, but rather be healed."

Hebrews 11, 39 to 12, 13.

In the eleventh chapter of this Epistle the Apostolic writer has been expounding the nature and function of faith in the actual life and witness of the great company of God's people who have gone before and who have now joined the Church triumphant which surrounds the throne of God in heaven, where Jesus Christ Himself is seated at the right hand of glory. It is in this communion of saints that we worship God, for when we come to Him we come to "the city of the living God, the heavenly Jerusalem, and to an innumerable company of angels, to the general assembly and church of the firstborn which are written in heaven, and to God the Judge of all, and to the spirits of just men made perfect, and to Jesus the mediator of the new covenant." But even throughout the whole life of faith on earth we are surrounded with this great cloud of witnesses. It is in that communion that faith has its beginning and its perfecting, all centred and grounded in Jesus.

In the opening of the twelfth chapter the writer has in his mind's eye the picture of a vast amphitheatre with its floor upon the earth and its sides reaching up into the heavens where they are packed with witnesses who have competed in the contest and finished their course. It is in that arena that the Christian community on earth is still engaged in the struggle—and the word that writer uses for "struggle" is the Greek word *agony* which describes the desperate agonising efforts of the athlete to win the race or triumph in the contest. The Christian life is an athletic "agony" in the arena of faith in which he is encouraged to run with patience when surrounded by the unseen host of the redeemed. But immediately the writer's thought leaps to the anguished agony of Jesus, who endured the Cross, despised the shame, and is now set down at the right hand of God's throne above. It is not the Christian athlete but Jesus Christ the great divine Agonist who holds the focus of attention, for all the witnesses

L

that surround the arena have their faces turned toward Him. It is the agony of His Cross endured with joy that rivets their gaze. It is because all eyes are turned toward Him, the Forerunner and Perfecter of faith, that the Christian athlete on earth is inspired to look away from himself to Jesus. He the Captain of salvation has already won the race and been crowned in triumph and the Christian athlete has only to run in the wake of His victory.

Then the writer says: "Consider him who endured so great an opposition of sinners to himself, lest you be wearied and faint in your minds." No doubt you find the Christian life of faith a struggle, in fact a real "agony", but look away from yourselves to Jesus and His agony. Set your life side by side with the agonising struggle and triumph of Jesus; and if you see that in its proper relation to your life, far from being dispirited and weary you will find your own life surging forward to its glorious fulfilment in Him.

(1) *The patience of Jesus*

It is the patience of One who endured gainsaying and contradiction and opposition heaped up endlessly upon Him but who suffered it all in sheer joy while throughout His love remained ever the same. The joy with which Christ endured the Cross is an element we frequently forget. Nothing can constitute a worse betrayal of Christ in His agony than to paint it over in romantic colours and to turn it into a thing of aesthetic beauty, when all the time it was the most dastardly and diabolical wickedness that black hell could conceive and establish on earth. But it is also a betrayal of His agony to rob Him of His joy in which He ate up the bread of affliction for the love of sinners. The Cross repels and attracts us alike in its terribleness, resisting all who come to offer their sympathy and admiration, but attracting all who come to yield the tribute of their shame and penitence. But none can worship the Man of sorrows aright unless he finds in His agony the one divine source on earth of ineffable joy and beauty.

It is that joyful endurance and patience of Jesus that is the source of our consolation and inspiration.

There are times, too many times doubtless, when we are overwhelmed in the struggles of life with the sense of defeat, and failure, and, it may be, even wonder whether we have exhausted at last the patience of God. We think of the ancient parable from the Old Testament reflected more than once in the parables of Jesus. "My beloved hath a vineyard on a very fruitful hill: he fenced it, and gathered out the stones thereof, and planted it with the choicest vine, and built a tower in the midst of it, and also made a wine-press therein And he looked that it should bring forth grapes, and it brought forth wild grapes. And now, I pray you, saith the Lord, judge between me and my vineyard. What could have been done more unto my vineyard that I have not done unto it?" Have we never felt that God must be baffled like that about us? Then let us turn our eyes to Jesus, looking away from ourselves to consider Him who endured such gainsaying of sinners against Himself, and we will learn there at the Cross that God refuses to accept any rebuff. They insulted Jesus, spat upon Him, flogged Him, mocked Him, and heaped all the obloquy and ignominy that fiendish ingenuity could devise, and crucified Him, and even when He was hanging by His nailed hands and feet from the Cross they tormented Him and cast His own words into His teeth. "Physician heal thyself. If thou be the Son of God come down from the cross, and we will believe." But the joy of Jesus in endurance was not exhausted, and His patience outlasted it all, and even outdid in love the contradiction of sinners against Him.

That belongs to the very marrow of the Gospel—the unwearied patience of the Lord Jesus with sinners. When we are tempted to grow weary and faint in our minds, let us consider Jesus, the incarnate patience of God, and learn to stake all our hope and trust on Him alone. Our only hope of salvation does rest upon this fact that God's love does not vary with our ups and downs. His love is absolutely unchanging and loves us most, if that were possible, when we are most contrary and rebellious. We may prove faithless, and fail again and again. We may grow weary of loving and become stricken with the sense of our own unworthiness, but here is the one solid unchanging fact upon which we can stand even when we are at the very end of our tether: God's patience is never at an end; the love of Jesus Christ does not grow weary of being love, no matter how shamefully we treat it. God's love will not cease to squander itself on faithless men and women, for it never grows tired of its indescribable compassion. It is forbearing love that knows no rebuff and outlives every contradiction of sin, love that patiently waits to be gracious. Let us therefore keep our eyes fixed on the unchanging and incarnate patience of God—Jesus Christ, the same yesterday, today and for ever.

(2) *Jesus the Captain and Perfecter of faith*

Jesus is the Author of our Salvation, but what He began to do He has completed. It is a finished work, which He has once and for all carried out, and which does not need and indeed cannot be repeated. It is because He has already completed the work which He set out to do that we may have such entire confidence in Him.

At this point the author of this Epistle refers back to teaching about Jesus which he had given earlier, when he wrote about Jesus as the Captain of our salvation made perfect through sufferings, and as learning obedience in the things that He suffered. This does not mean that in some way Jesus was morally and spiritually imperfect, and needed to be made perfect before He could become our Saviour. Nor does it mean that He had to be taught by hard suffering how to be obedient to the Father. God forbid. Jesus is the sinless and perfect Son of God. But He the Son of God has entered into the midst of our sinful humanity, identifying Himself to the utmost with us in our sinful life, yet without sin Himself. When He the holy One of God entered into our life like that He was met by the full assault of our temptations, and by the full contradiction of sinners against Him. He entered into the midst of man's contradiction of God and God's conflict with man, and took that contradiction and conflict upon Himself bearing it in His own heart and life in order to save us. Therefore when He met the full opposition of our enmity to God in the flesh, instead of retreating out of it again, Jesus endured it with joy; He laid hold upon sinners in His love, refusing to let them go, judging their sin, and reconciling them to God through His own blood. He so identified Himself with sinners that far from becoming a sinner Himself, He sanctified them by His union with them, and so the saving relationship with sinners upon which He embarked in His incarnation He brought to completion in the Cross. He had come to participate in the life of men in all their weakness and infirmity that they might participate in the life of the Son of God. He had come to identify Himself with us in all our guilty estrangement and distance from the Father, that we might be identified with Him in His relations with the Father, and in Him, through His very flesh, draw near to God with joy and boldness and without fear.

That was no easy task for Jesus. It was a desperate, anguished struggle that drew from Him strong crying and tears, and was fraught with fearful agony, but He achieved it. He broke a way through the fetters of sin and death by all that He suffered in His own flesh; and by bringing His self-identification with sinners and His participation in their life to completion, He carried them in Himself back into the presence of the Father and restored them to Him in glory. Jesus is, therefore, not only the Captain of salvation who opens up a new way through our hostility back to God, but the One who actually completes the work by uniting us to Himself and consecrating us together with Himself before God. He is the Author and the Perfecter of faith.

Two things especially we must lay to heart here. (*a*) In bringing His work to completion Jesus laid hold of man at the very point where he contradicts Him. Until we recognise that, and allow it to awaken in our own heart the recognition of the same antagonism within us to the love of God, we are evading the issue and destroying the relevance of the Cross to us. In other words, the Love of God lays hold upon us and exerts its power upon us by exposing in our hearts a deep-seated hostility to God. Is not the Cross God's attack upon the pride and inhumanity of man, and is it not man's attack upon the holiness and love of God? Jesus did not endure the Cross that we might side-step that whole issue between God and man, but endured the Cross both to expose our strange hatred of His grace and in grace to remove that antagonism through atonement. But He knows that this antagonism has its roots so deep in man's heart and will, and even beyond it in a vast evil will, that man is helpless to remove it. His will has become so much his self-will that whatever he does to escape from it only serves to imprison him deeper in his self-will. Man's hostility to God is part of a whole kingdom of evil over which he has no control. Jesus descended into that to do battle with it, to wrestle with it and to break its power over man, and to hew a way out of its tyranny and lead men back into the freedom of God's children.

He who refuses to acknowledge that the hostility that nailed Jesus to the Cross is lodged in his own heart, that he too has his full share in the contradiction of sinners against the love of God, renounces the relevance of the Cross to him, and puts himself beyond its saving power. Only if we are implicated in the Cross can it be an instrument for our salvation. Only when we allow it to uncover our guilty implication in the crucifixion of the Son of God, and to awaken in us the conviction that in our heart too there is embedded the contradiction of sin against God's love, does the Cross exert its healing power upon us. Then it is our Cross and our salvation, for we belong to the sinners who crucified Him and we belong to those for whom He died.

Take the romantic idea of the Cross as a picture of love, the view that refuses to see in it man's hatred for God's grace, but sees in it only the beautiful act of love dying for an ideal— is it true that the beauty of it, the moral influence of it, will purge the soul of man from his coarseness and redeem him? What picture of beauty or of love by its moral influence can save a soul or forgive a sinner or still the raging fire of conscience, or destroy the despair of the man who fails again and again and cannot cease failing? What relevance is there between beauty and forgiveness? Does anyone who has done some friend a shameful deed, betake himself to the Art Gallery in order to be forgiven? Or does any man whose soul is burning with horrible remorse and contempt and self-hatred recover the purity of love he has outraged by gazing at sweet innocent little children? Is it not the case that all that may even deepen the hostility of sin and drive a man rather to utter and complete despair?

That is why it is so important to be absolutely honest with the Cross of Jesus, to look at it without romanticising it, to face its challenge without evading its revelation of the depths of our heart, without letting the sin of deception drag us down and intensify our agony. There is only one place to look where our eyes can be cleansed from all deceit, and only one place to look in the agony of remorse or disaster, the Cross of Christ. And there is only one way to look at it: to look at it until we see in it the contradiction of our own heart to the love of God, and then to see that it is at that very point, at our very worst and vilest, that Jesus has laid hold of us and is most patient with us.

(*b*) In bringing His work to completion, Jesus reveals that He has already forged a unity between us and Himself which we do not need to achieve, but which we are to take in trust, in patient reliance upon Him. This is the astonishing message of this Epistle. It is not that Christ has once and for all wrought out our salvation, and that until we appropriate it, until we achieve unity with it, it is not real. Christ has already identified Himself with us not only in His incarnation but in the Cross, so that when He died He did not die as an isolated individual, or simply as the Leader. He so bound Himself to us that when He died we died in Him and with Him, and when He rose again we rose in Him and with Him, and when He presents Himself before the face of God He presents us also in Him before God. There are no words in our human language to declare that simple but profound mystery of unity with Christ adequately. It is a oneness with Him which He has already completed, and therefore we do not need to achieve it; it has already been achieved for us. It is already real, and we do not need to make it real. Certainly we must identify ourselves with Christ, and accept Him as the Saviour who died on our behalf, but when we do that aright, we rely upon a final and completed work. If we do not accept Christ as our Saviour, if we are not ready to identify ourselves with the sinners who crucified Him, and so with those whom He died to save, then certainly we exclude ourselves from the saving power of the Cross, and continue to oppose the love of God by contradicting its supreme act in the patience of Jesus. But if we do not accept Christ crucified as our Saviour, we do not undo the fact that He died for us;

we do not make it unreal that He has wrought out our
salvation; we dash ourselves against the Cross, and bring the
judgment of His blood upon our heads. To resist the ultimate
out-pouring of the Love of God on the Cross, is to meet the
wrath of the Lamb.

(3) *Consider Jesus*

Jesus Christ Himself must always be the supreme object
of our meditation and faith if we are not to grow weary and
faint in our souls. We are reminded here of the virgin Mary
who kept all the things she was told about her infant child in
her heart and pondered them there, turning them over and
over in her innermost thoughts. Among the things that she
pondered like that were the words of Simeon about Jesus,
that child though He was He was set for the falling and rising
again of many in Israel, and for a sign that would be contradicted, that the thoughts of many hearts might be revealed.
That is how we too are to consider Jesus who endured such
contradiction of sinners against Himself, carefully taking to
our hearts and considering His whole life of patient love and
joyful endurance, and, behold, the thoughts of our own hearts
are thereby revealed—and cleansed.

But the apostolic writer has more than that in mind, for
he has picked his expression with care. To consider Jesus is
to place our lives along side of His, to bring our lives and Jesus
into "analogy", and to think of ourselves only in Him.
Certainly that means that we are to "imitate" Jesus, to take up
our Cross and follow Him in His patient endurance of all
that so severely contradicted and opposed His love—but it is
more than that. Because He has already identified Himself
with us and suffered in our place, and endured our contradiction of Him, when we place our lives under the light of
His suffering, we find that they take their character from Him,
and that His patient endurance and joy are imprinted upon us,

so that we begin to reflect the image of His love and patience.

It is the same thought, for example, as St. Paul expounded, writing from prison, to the Philippians, when he encouraged them to let the mind that was in Christ be in them, the mind of the Christ who, though He was God, abased Himself and became a servant, and was obedient unto the death of the Cross; or when speaking of himself Paul declared that his sole aim was to know Jesus Christ, and know Him in the power of His resurrection, but that meant knowing Him in the fellowship of His sufferings. That is what the writer has in mind here. Because of what Christ has already done for us in Himself, we are privileged in all our suffering, in resisting sin, to have fellowship with the sufferings of Christ. But if we suffer with Him, we shall also reign with Him. If we look at our suffering in Him, and look upon it as a means of sharing in His suffering, then it will be to us a pledge of our sharing in His victory. Far from being wearied or dispirited, we shall then be refreshed and quickened in the contest of faith, and be encouraged to greater resistence, striving against sin.

Moreover, if the whole focus of our vision is directed toward Christ and we consider the whole of His patience from the beginning to its ending, from His inauguration of the course of faith to His consummation of it, we shall find that He is the link between what has already happened in us and what is yet to be fulfilled. With the coming of Jesus a new era began, which will not come to an end, but which reaches out beyond to the perfect Kingdom of God. It is Jesus Christ Himself who is the link between this age and the age to come, between us here and now on earth in the struggle of faith, and the goal of our life in God. What He has begun in us He will certainly consummate in us, for He has already perfected it in Himself for us. It was not for Himself that He died and rose again, but for us. In Himself He has already perfected the whole course of faith, so that in Him we have already run the race, and attained the goal victoriously. There-fore if we find that there is still a great deal of sin in our lives to resist, if we are tempted to think that we have made no progress in battling against it but still are where we were long ago, then let us look away from ourselves altogether to Jesus and be absolutely assured that He is not only the Leader and Captain of our salvation but the Perfecter and Consum-mator of the whole course of faith. He who endured on the Cross all the enmity of man's heart towards God, and endured it with a joy and love that outlasts the very worst that sin can do, will certainly not fail us in this age or in the age to come. Wherefore, consider Him who endured such contra-diction of sinners against Himself, lest we grow weary or faint in our minds.

CHAPTER III

THE MEDIATOR OF THE
NEW COVENANT

"Ye are not come unto a mount that might be touched, and that burned with fire, and unto blackness, and darkness, and tempest, and the sound of a trumpet, and the voice of words; which voice they that heard intreated that no word more should be spoken unto them: for they could not endure that which was enjoined, If even a beast touch the mountain, it shall be stoned; and so fearful was the appearance, that Moses said, I exceedingly fear and quake: but ye are come unto Mount Zion, and unto the city of the living God, the heavenly Jerusalem, and to innumerable hosts of angels, and to the general assembly and church of the firstborn who are enrolled in heaven, and to God the judge of all, and to the spirits of just men made perfect, and to Jesus the mediator of a new covenant, and to the blood of sprinkling that speaketh better than that of Abel. See that ye refuse not him that speaketh."   Hebrews 12, 18-25.

In these verses the Word of God speaks to us of the blessedness and joy of our salvation in Jesus Christ in contrast to the darkness and terror of Mt. Sinai. "You are not come unto the Mount that might be touched, and that burned with fire . . . but you are come to Jesus the Mediator of the New Covenant, and to the blood of sprinkling . . ." Here, on the one hand, then, we have the Old Testament with its thunder and smoke and fire and the reek of a thousand thousand sacrifices; but on the other hand we have the New Testament with its figure of the wonderful Saviour, and that stain of blood on the little hill outside Jerusalem that speaks more potently than all the trumpet-blasts of the Old Testament.

That does not mean that the Old Testament is only the record of a crude and primitive religion, and that now its violence and harshness have to be set completely aside as something outmoded by the higher religion of love of the New Testament. On the contrary, the Old Testament is God's revelation; it is the record of the way which His infinite love took with a stubborn and rebellious people binding it into a covenant of mercy and truth with Himself, subjecting it to the ordeal of suffering and judgment which that covenant involved when Israel kicked against it, in order at last to prepare a place in Israel for the Incarnation of God's beloved Son. Moreover, the love of God is so infinite and so wonderful, and the blood of Christ is so holy, that we can understand it only through such a contrast as that between Sinai and Calvary, between judgment and mercy, between inexorable command and unstinting grace.

Let us recall, then, how the Old Covenant was founded at Mt. Sinai. For long years the tribes of Jacob had been buried in oblivion, and enslaved in tyranny, in Egypt. Then God sent Moses to be the instrument of their deliverance and the mediator of a covenant between God and the children of Israel in which they were to be transplanted out of Egypt

into a country of their own, and established as a nation under
the wings of the divine mercy. Hitherto their knowledge of
God and of what He was to do for them was communicated
to them only through Moses, but now they were to be
brought to meet with God at Mt. Sinai, where He was to
condescend to speak with them directly and they were to
listen to His voice. At last the moment came as the people
were assembled at Mt. Sinai. The earth quaked, thunderclaps
crashed round the camp, the lightning ripped open the skies,
and great trumpet-blasts tore through the frightened air, and
the presence of God descended in a thick cloud upon the
Mount and God spoke. Israel was stricken with terror. They
fled into their tents and fell down on their faces before the
awful sublimity of divine majesty and holiness. It was
unendurable, and even Moses himself feared and quaked
exceedingly. Divine as the voice was, it froze them with fear,
so that in sheer desperation they intreated that no such words
should be spoken unto them. "Speak thou with us," they said
to Moses, "and we will hear, but let not God speak to us, lest
we die." They were happy to go on worshipping God, they
were ready to obey His commandments, but to enter into
direct dialogue with God was more than they could face, for
God is a consuming fire. They did not know they would be
afraid of God until He actually spoke, then they were
mortally terrified, for it echoed in the accusations of their
own hearts as at the last judgment. They were too sinful to
listen to the naked voice of God. If God's voice was to come
to them, it must come through a mediator, come from a
distance through a messenger, through the commandments
of the law mediated by Moses, through the elaborate ritual
of the tabernacle, in which Aaron alone, the high priest,
should enter into the holy of holies within the veil to com-
mune with God, and then bring the Word of God back to the
people. And so it came to pass. The voice and presence of

God were mediated to Israel indirectly. The children of Israel exchanged immediate communion with God for bondage to carnal ordinances, as this Epistle calls them.

That is not what we come to in the New Testament and in the New Covenant. We do not come to the mount that can be touched and that burns with fire, but to the hill called Calvary, and to Jesus the Mediator of the New Covenant who is God Himself come near to us.

(1) *The New Approach*

The whole ground of religion has been altered; the fundamental basis of man's relation to God is changed. There is a new approach, a New Covenant and a New Testament. The ground of the Old Covenant at Mt. Sinai, the mountain of the law-giving, and the basis of approach to God was to be found in the fulfilment of God's holy command. It was a fearful command, as we have seen, and so dreaded was it that Moses had to act as a go-between between God and man, and a great curtain of religion was erected between them so that under its cover the people could draw as near to God as possible, but always on this side of the veil, where they would not be consumed by His majesty. But now under the New Covenant ratified in the blood of Christ, the ground of man's approach to God is not first a command by God but an act of sheer love in which God has given Himself to sinful man in such a way as to set man in the presence of God on the basis of forgiveness and peace. In other words, the basis of man's approach to God is not God's demand but a gift of sheer love. "God has so loved the world that He has given His only-begotten Son that whosoever believes in Him should not perish but have everlasting life." The presence of Jesus Christ in the world means that God's love has overtaken us, that God does not wait for men to approach Him. He anticipates them in the wonder of His grace. Like the father

in Jesus' parable of the lost son, God has come to meet us
when we are far off. He plies us with His love and mercy and
shows Himself on the side of frail human nature, gathering
us up in His arms of mercy and folding us to Himself in
everlasting love.

In the blood of Jesus Christ, God has established a New
Covenant in which God has once and for all committed
Himself to us in an act of sheer unstinting love, and so
bound Himself to us in love that He will not and cannot go
back on His Word. God has done a deed and spoken a final
Word which rends the darkness and dispels the terror of Mt.
Sinai, for in it He has pledged Himself in forgiveness and
pardon to all men, so that the weakest of us, the sinfullest of
us, may venture to go directly to God and receive His pardon
and mercy. And God will not alter the Word that has gone
out of His mouth or withdraw Himself from the deed of
mercy, for He has signed it with His own blood in the death
of Jesus. God is faithful and keeps His Word, and therefore
we may now approach Holy God in deepest reverence and
with joy to plead the blood of sprinkling. We may come
gladly, then, to the Table of the Lord, to handle in our
hands the broken body and the blood of Jesus, God's own
covenanted pledges. We may redeem those pledges simply by
taking them. We may come to take God at His Word. And
the fundamental basis for it all, the reason for our daring
to come to the Holy Mount, to the Table of the Lord, is
because God has eternally committed Himself to free pardon
and undeserved forgiveness through the blood of Christ.
The central fact here is not what we do, but what God has
already done and completed in His self-commitment to us on
the Cross. Let not our own unworthiness prevent us from
coming but rather be the reason for casting ourselves upon
His mercy. Because God has committed Himself to us like
that in pure uninhibited love, there is nothing in which we

can hurt Him more than in refusing to take Him at His Word. "See that you refuse not Him that speaketh."

(2) *The Mystery of Blood*

This is the holiest mystery of our faith, the blood of sprinkling. Many a man's blood has been shed for his fellows, but Jesus Christ stands quite apart, for His sacrifice is a lonely and terrible thing with an infinitely profounder meaning, so profound that to us it will ever remain a deep mystery. Even the Bible gives us no ultimate explanation of it. The Old Testament had its shedding of blood in sacrifice before God, but there the ultimate explanation is simply that God has given it in witness to His atoning mercy. In the New Testament it is the blood of the Son of God that is the blood of the covenant, and its ultimate explanation, as Jesus Himself told us, is to be found in the Will of the heavenly Father.

But think again of the contrast that is given to us in this twelfth chapter of Hebrews. Go back first to the picture of Moses at Mt. Sinai taking the part of the mediator between God and His rebellious children as he entered the thick cloud which shrouded the presence of God and out of which there came that unforgettable voice, until Moses feared and quaked exceedingly. Now go back to the Gospels and watch Jesus as He sets His face like a flint to turn toward the Cross, and listen to Him as He says: "I have a terrible baptism with which to be baptised, and how is my soul troubled until it is over." Watch Him as He prays in the Garden of Gethsemane, where the awful burden of our sin and its judgment presses down upon Him until He cries out in agony and tears, and great drops as of blood fall from His brow. Watch Him at last on the Cross entering the thick darkness of the world's sin and guilt and God's wrath poured out in judgment upon it, and hear those terrible words: "My God, my God, why hast thou forsaken me?"

It is Mt. Sinai that helps us to understand that. There a covenant was established between God and man in such a way that the barrier of the law and religious ritual stood in between God and man to hold them apart as it were, and so to protect the sinner from the holiness of God, as well as to mediate between them. The law and the ritual bound God and man together, for they told man what God required of him and what kind of response he was to make to God in fulfilment of the covenant, but all the time God and man were separated by the veil. Only symbolically, only in religious ceremonies could man come into the presence of God, but those ceremonies and sacrifices could not take away man's sin and the law could not justify man in God's sight—but they did point forward to a better hope when at last the veil would be taken away and man and God would be reconciled for ever. Until that happened, the law and the cult were the means by which the children of Israel were mercifully protected from utter judgment and through which they learned that God is faithful to His promises of mercy and pardon.

In Jesus God Himself has come among men to be His own Mediator and our Mediator. All through His life, but above all in His death on the Cross, Jesus penetrated the veil that divides disobedient man from God, the veil that is woven by man's sin on one side, and by God's judgment upon it on the other side. He stood in the gap between God's wrath and man's guilt, and by enduring and offering as God and Man all that was righteous and true He destroyed the barrier and effected reconciliation between God and man. He was God the Son standing in our place and bearing the just judgment on our iniquity. He was also Man wearing our humanity and offering to God in our place and what we could not offer, a perfect offering of obedience and faithfulness. He was God descending into our abysmal wickedness and laying hold of us in it in sheer love, and He was man laying

M

hold of God by submitting obediently to the divine judgment of sinful man. And so on the Cross, Jesus entered into the horror of great darkness which Moses and Israel could not bear at Sinai, and sacrificed Himself as an offering well-pleasing to God, and shed His blood in expiation for our sin.

Words cannot suffice to speak of this holy mystery, but where our words fail, the Lord has given us the sacrament of His broken body and shed blood, which make unmistakably clear that through the body and blood of our Saviour we have peace with God and are given to share by the power of the Holy Spirit in the communion between the Father and the Son. The sophisticated and proud lovers of beauty may well be scandalised by the place which the blood of Christ occupies in our faith, but it is the poor sinner passing through the waters of death, the wounded conscience that will not be stilled, the penitent who at Holy Communion can only offer to Christ the tribute of their shame, that understand this mystery, that the blood of Jesus Christ cleanses us from all sin.

(3) *The Voice of Love*

Out of the darkness of Calvary there comes now not the unbearable voice of Sinai, but the voice of incredible love: "Father, forgive them, for they know not what they do." It is the voice of love and mercy and pardon coming right out of the heart of judgment. That is why it is such wonderful love.

One of the things that strikes us again and again as we read the pages of the New Testament is that this Jesus who stooped to share our lot and who speaks and acts with such tender pity and compassion to sinners is none other than the Lord God, the God of the Old Testament as well as the God of the New, the Creator as well as the Redeemer, yes, the God of Sinai as well as the God of Calvary.

Many modern readers of the Gospels have been puzzled

by what they think to be two divergent accounts of Jesus. On the one hand, there is "the Jesus of forked-lightning", for no one ever spoke such scorching words as He, or spoke with such majesty and authority as He spoke. But, on the other hand, there is "the Jesus of the Galilean idyll", the Jesus of idyllic calm and peace whose kindness called forth such amazement, for people wondered at the gracious words that fell from His lips. Now it is the blood of the Cross that makes us see that those two are one, and it is out of that oneness that there comes the voice of everlasting love and mercy, of infinite pity and grace. And this is the profoundest mystery of it: the voice that comes out of the heart of Calvary speaking forgiveness and love is the same voice that spoke on Mt. Sinai, and it is because of the blood of the Son of God that it is the same voice.

Look at it like this. Unless the voice of forgiving love is identical with the accusing voice that echoes in our conscience we cannot trust it. It would be a counterfeit voice or a fiction. Only when the one who condemns us forgives us are we liberated from fear into perfect love. That is why the Cross speaks so eloquently of God's love, because of the blood of Christ. Because of this blood which tells us that the God of Sinai and of our conscience has come Himself to forgive in sheer unmitigated love at cost only to Himself, we can come to Him without any fear whatsoever. Who wants now to listen to the thunder of Sinai when the voice of Christ's blood cries from the ground? Who is he that condemneth? It is Christ that died!

Here in the Cross we are assured that God does not sit apart in the hidden exaltation of Sinai as a mere Spectator or Arbiter of human affairs, watching our struggles and noting our falls. No! here into the long struggle of men, into their abject failure, there has entered One who is God manifest in pure love, and who has laid upon His heart the whole burden of our smitten conscience and shame, and whose whole concern is our restoration to the joyous and guiltless freedom of God's children.

No wonder, then, that the earliest disciples who first heard this voice spoke in such terms of the death of Jesus. "There is therefore now no condemnation to them that are in Christ Jesus." "The blood of Jesus Christ God's Son cleanses from all sin." "He loved me and gave himself for me." And so through their witness the voice of God's amazing love continues to speak.

That is the very voice we hear speaking to us today out of the dark mystery of Golgotha, the voice of unreserved pardon and unstinting love. It is only out of the agony of the Cross that we can hear that voice in a way that entirely banishes guilt and fear. Just how that is made possible through the blood of Christ we can never fully fathom, but this is absolutely clear, that the death of Christ is ever present to the mind and heart of the Father and in and through it the whole heart and mind of the Father is directed toward us in a covenant of pure love and grace in which each of us is bidden to share so that each of us can say in the words of St. Paul: "He loved me, and gave himself for me."

CHAPTER IV

THE TRINITY OF LOVE

"This is the third time I am coming to you. At the mouth of two witnesses or three shall every word be established. I have said beforehand, and I do say beforehand, as when I was present the second time, so now, being absent, to them that have sinned heretofore, and to all the rest, that, if I come again, I will not spare; seeing that ye seek a proof of Christ that speaketh in me; who to

you-ward is not weak, but is powerful in you: for he was crucified
through weakness, yet he liveth through the power of God. For
we also are weak in him, but we shall live with him through the
power of God toward you. Try your own selves, whether ye be in
the faith; prove your own selves. Or know ye not as to your own
selves, that Jesus Christ is in you? unless indeed ye be reprobate.
But I hope that ye shall know that we are not reprobate. Now we
pray to God that ye do no evil; not that we may appear approved,
but that ye may do that which is honourable, though we be as
reprobate. For we can do nothing against the truth, but for the
truth. For we rejoice, when we are weak, and ye are strong: this we
also pray for, even your perfecting. For this cause I write these
things while absent, that I may not when present deal sharply,
according to the authority which the Lord gave me for building up,
and not for casting down.

"Finally, brethren, farewell. Be perfected; be comforted; be of
the same mind; live in peace: and the God of love and peace shall
be with you. Salute one another with a holy kiss.

"All the saints salute you.

"The grace of the Lord Jesus Christ, and the love of God, and
the communion of the Holy Ghost, be with you all."

II Corinthians 13.

In the calendar of the Christian Church Trinity Sunday
comes after *Easter, Ascension* and *Pentecost.* At Easter we
remember especially the death and resurrection of the *Lord
Jesus Christ* from the dead; at Ascension we remember that,
He ascended to the right hand of *God the Father Almighty*;
and at Pentecost, or Whitsunday as we call it, we remember
that God has poured out His *Holy Spirit* upon the Church.
Now, immediately following Whitsunday is Trinity Sunday,
in which we meditate upon the fact that Father, Son and
Holy Spirit are One God. God is a Holy Trinity of three
Persons, but that does not mean that God is composed of
three separated individuals. It means that while God is
three Persons, Father, Son and Holy Spirit, they are not
separated from one another like human persons. They are
Three in One. That is such a high and wonderful mystery

that even the greatest theologians can only speak very stammeringly about it.

And yet the New Testament does speak very simply about the Holy Trinity, and it is one of these simple statements that we are to meditate upon now. "The grace of the Lord Jesus Christ, and the love of God, and the communion of the Holy Spirit be with you all." Notice that it speaks of the Trinity as the *grace* of Christ, the *love* of God, and the *communion* of the Holy Spirit. It is a *Trinity of Love*.

With these words St. Paul concludes the most intimate and humiliating and self-revealing of all his epistles. A number of his Corinthian converts had questioned his apostleship and treated him with contempt in order to cloak their own errors and justify themselves. Paul meets this in the most astounding way. He pleads with them as a father with his own children, rebukes them and yet spares them. He boasts of them as his own commendation and glory, and finds himself also compelled "foolishly" to boast of all that he has suffered—and what a catalogue of affliction that was!—on their behalf and for the sake of the Gospel, and so from beginning to end he pours out his soul in such a way that it is abundantly clear that his whole life is bound up with that of his spiritual children. When they live, he lives; when it goes wrong with them, he is devastated. And throughout all Paul abases himself in his readiness to suffer attack and reproach and shame, if only his beloved converts may be kept true to the faith that is in Christ Jesus. He acknowledges frankly that he is indeed, as they say, weak and contemptible in his own person. God means them to see him like that, he says, that they may not mistake the earthen vessel for the heavenly treasure, but he reminds them too that God in His amazing grace has abased Himself in Christ that we might be exalted, and so He elects to use the weak and base things of this world as the instruments of His love and power. But if the weakness of Christ is the power of God, then Paul glories in his weakness in God that he may also be strong in God, but he is ready in all his own infirmities to be weak with the weakness of God for the Corinthians' sake, that they may be strong in the grace of God.

As a seal to this epistle, summing up its teaching and as a prayerful salutation to the Corinthians he ends with these words: "The grace of the Lord Jesus Christ, and the love of God, and the Communion of the Holy Spirit, be with you all. Amen." These words, the most frequently cited of all that the Apostle wrote, give us at once the fullest and simplest statement about the Holy Trinity, but they are given not as a statement of high speculative theology but as a statement of the condescension of God to our weakness, that we through the weakness of God may be exalted to live with Him, in the *grace* of Christ, the *love of* God, and the *communion* of the Holy Spirit. He is a *Trinity of Love.*

(1) *The grace of the Lord Jesus Christ*

That certainly refers to the *graciousness* of Jesus. Was ever anyone more gracious than He? The Evangelists tell us that the crowds were astonished at the gracious words that fell from His lips, the common people heard Him gladly, and all alike acknowledged His unlimited kindness, His infinite compassion, His incredible love that would not grow weary of loving; even when He was harshly rebuffed, spat upon, whipped and crucified, He loved to the very end, and loved to the utmost: and all with such grace and tender pity that every time we read about it in the Gospels it takes our breath away.

But the grace of the Lord Jesus means more than that— "Ye know the grace of the Lord Jesus," said St. Paul, "that though He was rich, yet for your sakes He became poor, that ye through His poverty might become rich." That is the incredible fact about the grace of Christ, the wondrous exchange that He offers us. He who had no need, the Holy Son of God, came down where we are in all our sin and shame and guilt under the judgment of God, and took our place, that we might be given His place. Every man must give to God an account for what he has done; every man must face the bar of the divine judgment, stand in the light of God's pure scrutiny and reveal the hidden impurities and betrayals of his life. But what man is there who can look into the face of God and live? His holy Love would only uncover our unloveliness and sin, and we could only come under its utter condemnation. But Jesus stood in our place, and bearing the load of our sin and shame, and all our guilt, He faced the bar of the divine judgment and was judged, the Just for the unjust, the Righteous for the sinner. That was the poverty of Jesus on the Cross, when all that He had He freely yielded up to us—He was clothed with our shame, that we might be clothed with His glory: that is the meaning of the grace of the Lord Jesus Christ.

The Word of God speaks to us here as those for whom Jesus died in shame and judgment. God, our Maker and our heavenly Father, summons us to give to Him an account of our life, and to reveal our heart and soul to the eyes of His purity and love, and asks of us the obedience of our whole life in body and soul.

What are we to do in answer to God? This is just the point where Jesus comes and says to us: What you dare not do, and what you cannot do, I have done already, and done for you. I stood in your place and have given to God an account for your sin and guilt and shame. I owned up to it all for you and received God's righteous judgment upon it all. Where you were disobedient, I was obedient, for you; where you were impure, I offered to God a pure heart, for you; where you were untrue and false, where you betrayed God's Holy Love,

I remained true to the very end, for you. I loved you and gave Myself for you.

That is why Jesus is constantly calling us to bring our burdens to Himself that He may give us rest, and promises that He will turn none away. "Come unto me all ye that labour and are heavy laden, and I will give you rest." He has come to shoulder our awful burden of responsibility to God for our sin and to give us pardon and rest; He has come to bear our weakness and our unfaithfulness and to give us strength in being yoked to Him. "Take my yoke upon you," Jesus says, "and learn of me; for I am meek and lowly in heart and ye shall find rest unto your souls." Jesus knows that we are unable to give an account to God or to make a decision for Him, but He has done that for us and He asks us to trust Him. Jesus knows we have been unfaithful and can hardly believe, but He remains utterly faithful and He asks us to rely on Him for He will never fail us.

We may be among those who, perhaps in a recent evangelistic crusade or mission, have made our decision for Christ, offering to God our body and soul. But let us remember that, long before we did that, Jesus made the decision for us, and He asks us not to trust our own decision but to trust Him. Our decision is like the act of putting our hand in His, for it is He who has laid hold of us, and certainly He will hold us fast and will never let us go. There are many others, however, who have never given themselves decisively to God like that, and they know that they have no strength to do it. No matter how much evangelists or friends plead with them to do it, they cannot get past their own weakness, and indeed the more they are challenged to undertake an act of will upon which the whole of their eternal salvation will depend, the more they stagger at its impossibility and are driven into despair or incredulity. Tell them rather the whole Gospel of the grace of Christ, that it belongs to His grace that He has already made the great decision for them, and now invites them to rely upon His prior decision, and so to throw their lot in with Him, and let Him yoke them to His true decision and to His absolute faithfulness. Let the sinner learn to glory in his very weakness that the Power of Christ may rest upon him.

The great Apostle tells us that God left him a thorn in his flesh just to keep him humble and remind him of his weakness, and though St. Paul besought the Lord three times to take it away, He answered: "My grace is sufficient for thee: for my strength is made perfect in weakness." And Paul himself adds: "Most gladly therefore will I rather glory in my infirmities, that the power of Christ may rest upon me. When I am weak, then am I strong."

Here let us recall the fact of our Baptism in all the helplessness of infancy. Let no man despise the weakness of the infant at the holy Font where it is signed and sealed as a little child for whom Christ died and rose again, for it is just in that helplessness that God's strength is made perfect, and in that weakness that the grace of Christ is most gloriously manifested. Let us therefore glory in our Baptism, for it remains as the sacred sign to remind us that long before we could make any decision for Christ, His grace laid hold of us, and that even now when we are enabled to make our decision for Christ, it is in our weakness that we are to glory and not in our strength. Let Baptism still proclaim to us that we belong to Christ, that we are not our own, for He has bought us with His precious blood; and let it continue to teach us to put our trust in Christ as our personal Saviour and to rely entirely upon that which Baptism has extended and sealed to us: the grace of the Lord Jesus Christ.

(2) *And the love of God*

The Gospel does not stop at the grace of the Lord Jesus

Christ, it goes on to speak of the love of God. If it did not go on to speak of the love of God, the Gospel would only be a beautiful story with no eternity in it.

Look at it like this: the Gospel story of the kindness and grace of Jesus is wonderful beyond all telling. But was it only the story of a man, a very wonderful man? Is the Gospel only a piece of bygone history, that happened once upon a time? Is that all there is to it? Not at all. This Jesus ascended to the right hand of God the Father Almighty and that tells us that the grace of the Lord Jesus is identical with the love of God. All that is most wonderful in the Gospel story is an account of the eternal love of the eternal God. The love of Jesus for us, what Jesus did for us, is not just a passing episode in history, a beautiful piece of tragic drama. On the contrary, it was the eternal love of God come down in human form: and therefore what Jesus has done for us is eternal. It is everlasting. It is absolutely divine. It will never pass away, never fail, never be undone. The kindness and graciousness of Jesus is the incarnate love of the Eternal God.

Look at it the other way round. What is the love of God? The love of God means that God made us for Himself, that God will not be without us. The love of God means that He gives Himself to us. He wants to be ours, and He wants us to be His. God's love is the giving of Himself to men. But are we not afraid of the love of God? God is holy, pure, true, utterly and only Love. Are we prepared for God to give Himself to us, for His holy, pure love to be a living presence in our heart and life? Is that not just what we are afraid of? If God in His love gives Himself to me, His love would burn up my self-love; His purity would attack my impurity; His truth would slay my falsehood and hypocrisy. The love of God would be my judgment. God's love is wrath against all self-love. God's love is a consuming fire against all that is unloving and selfish and sinful. If I am to receive the love of God it can only be in abject repentance and self-denial.

That is why we are afraid of God—because He wants to give Himself to us in love, and His love is our judgment. Because we are afraid, our guilty conscience distorts the face of God for us and makes us afraid to look upon Him. We are trapped in the pit of our own fears, and run away from the very One who really loves and the only One who can forgive us.

Now listen to the message of this verse: the love of God is identical with the grace of the Lord Jesus Christ. Look at Jesus Christ, look at His wonderful graciousness and kindness, and keep looking at Him until you realise that there is no other God but Christ: that the grace of Christ is the eternal love of God at work among sinners. Watch Jesus and see how He deals with sinners; how, for example, He dealt with the woman taken in adultery, with Zacchaeus the tax-gatherer, or with Peter in his base denial. The love of Jesus is certainly the most devastating judgment upon our sin, but it is sheer unmitigated love, and infinitely kind and tender: but that is the eternal love of God.

In the Bible there is a remarkable word used to speak of the merciful love of God, which comes from the Hebrew word for the womb, and which speaks of the tender pity which a mother has toward her unborn babe. The love of God is like that. In Jesus Christ the Son of God has become one body with us, and loves us with a depth of tenderness and compassion infinitely more wonderful than that of a mother toward her unborn baby.

The grace of the Lord Jesus Christ is to be understood only when we see that it is identical with the eternal love of God, but the measure of that eternal love of God poured out upon us in utter compassion is to be understood only by the infinite extent of God's condescension in the abasement and poverty of Jesus upon the Cross. We say far, far too easily that the Cross is the manifestation of the love of God. Is it? Take one of the really great paintings of the crucifixion of Christ, of Holbein or of Grünewald, which has depicted the crucifixion in all its truth and stark actuality. Put a magnifying glass upon the canvas and look closely at the black, lacerated flesh, at the unutterable wickedness inflicted upon the Son of Man, and you recoil in utter horror—it is too terrible to look at; it is quite unendurable. That is the manifestation of fiendish wickedness and diabolical hatred, a manifestation of man's bitter hatred of God's grace. It is the uncovering of sin in all its abysmal iniquity. How can we say that the Cross is the supreme manifestation of the love of God, when to look at it threatens to destroy our faith in God because He allowed the one holy and pure Man who ever lived to suffer such untold shame and ignominy, and threatens also to destroy our faith in man, for man is so unutterably bad that he rose up, spat in the face of the Son of God and slew Him on a tree? The Cross is indeed the manifestation of the love of God, but only when we see that God endured all that for our sakes, that God abased Himself to suffer and bear the vileness of our sin, that He might freely forgive us at cost only to Himself. The Cross is the manifestation of God's love because in it God has poured Himself out in infinite compassion upon man at his vilest, in order to gather him back into the communion of His divine love.

It is the Cross that persuades us that God loves us with an infinite and eternal love. Therefore when our heart condemns us, when our conscience is set on fire of hell, when in our bones there burns the fire of remorse which no human word can quench, let the Cross of Christ persuade us of this, that God loves us with an everlasting love and will not let us go. In His love there is room even for me.

(3) The Communion of the Holy Spirit

John Calvin used to speak of the Communion of the Holy Spirit as "the sacred conjugal union" in which God binds us to Himself in Jesus Christ. When a man and a woman are yoked together in a covenant of love and by act of God are made one for ever, that is but a pale reflection of what God wants to do with us in the Communion of the Holy Spirit. Through this communion we are yoked together with Jesus Christ in love, and are for ever made to share with Him in the riches of His grace in the love of God. Apart from that union with Christ through the power of the Spirit, all that the Gospel has to say of the grace of the Lord Jesus and the love of God would be useless to us. The Communion of the Spirit is the bond of love which actually binds us to God and makes us share in the grace of Jesus Christ.

Behind all that we hear in the Gospel lies the fact that in creating man God willed to share His glory with man and willed man to have communion with Himself; it is the fact of the overflowing love of God that refused, so to speak, to be pent up within God, but insisted in creating a fellowship into which it could pour itself out in unending grace. Far from being rebuffed by the disobedience and rebellion of man, the will of God's love to seek and create fellowship with man established the covenant of grace in which God promised to man in spite of his sin to be His God, and insisted on binding man to Himself as His child and partner in love. God remained true and faithful to His covenant. He established it in the midst of the people of Israel, and all through their history God was patiently at work, preparing a way for the Incarnation of His love at last in Jesus Christ, that in and through Him He might bring His covenant to complete fulfilment and gather man back into joyful communion with Himself.

In Jesus Christ God fulfilled His covenant promise, giving Himself to man anew in the fellowship of grace, and reconciling man to Himself in the communion of love, but now that the covenant will of God is fulfilled in the midst of our humanity, and established once and for all in the blood of Christ, God has poured out His Spirit, and through His Spirit He pours out His love, into the hearts of His children. The bond of the covenant remains and is more steadfast than ever, but now in addition to the covenant, as its inner fulfilment, God bestows upon us the Communion of the Spirit in which He not only restores us to Himself but shares with us His divine life and love. The outward form which the Covenant takes in the New Testament is found in the holy Sacraments, the pledges of God's faithfulness, the signs and seals of fulfilled promises; the inward form which the Covenant takes is the Communion of the Spirit, through which we are taken up to share in the love of the Father and the Son and the Holy Spirit. This glorious inheritance is already ours in Christ, but only when He comes again in power and glory to renew the heaven and the earth will we enter into the fulness of this inheritance. Until then we are given the gift of the Spirit as a pledge and first-fruit of our inheritance; through this gift we are bound to the life of God, God's eternal love is shed abroad in our hearts, and we taste already the powers of the age to come. The gift of the Spirit is the pledge of the faithfulness of God, the miracle that in and through the crucified and risen Christ we have peace with God here and now and are quickened again with the life-giving breath of the Creator.

When the work of atonement was wrought out in His death and resurrection, when God and man were reconciled, Jesus returned to His disciples, and said "Peace be unto you." And when He had said that, He breathed on them and said "Receive ye the Holy Spirit. Whosesoever sins ye remit, they are remitted unto them, and whosesoever sins ye retain, they are retained." Wherever the Gospel of forgiveness and reconciliation is proclaimed, there Christ is present to all who gather into His name, to grant peace with God and to bestow the gift of the Holy Spirit. He shares with them the riches of His grace and the eternal love of God in the Communion of the Holy Spirit.

"The grace of the Lord Jesus Christ and the love of God and the communion of the Holy Spirit be with you all. Amen."